Edwin Carton Booth

Australia

Edwin Carton Booth

Australia

ISBN/EAN: 9783337413880

Printed in Europe, USA, Canada, Australia, Japan

Cover: Foto ©Andreas Hilbeck / pixelio.de

More available books at **www.hansebooks.com**

THE WORLD

BY EDWIN CARTON BOOTH, F.R.C.I.

ILLUSTRATED WITH
DRAWINGS BY SKINNER PROUT, N. CHEVALIER, Etc.

IN TWO VOLUMES
VOL. II.

LONDON: VIRTUE AND COMPANY, LIMITED

CONTENTS OF VOL. II.

CHAPTER XIV.

NEW SOUTH WALES (continued).

The River Hunter.—Newcastle.—The Towns up the River.—A New Industry.—Railway Extension.—The Mackony River.—The Clarence.—The Richmond.—The Far North of New South Wales 126

CHAPTER XV.

NEW SOUTH WALES (continued).

The First Explorers.—The Cow Pasture.—The Hawkesbury.—Early Rumours of Gold.—Overland to China.—The Western Railway.—The Parramatta River.—The Waterfalls.—Bathurst 133

CHAPTER XVI.

NEW SOUTH WALES (concluded).

South of Sydney.—Character of Country and People.—Varied Employments—Fishing.—Randwick.—Illawarra.—Forest Trees.—Wollongong.—Shoalhaven.—Ulladulla.—The Rhomboid of Monaro 142

CHAPTER XVII.

QUEENSLAND.

Systematic Emigration; its Failure.—A Guarantee of Success.—Early Condition of Queensland.—The Survey of Flinders.—The Natives; their Treatment.—Convicts' Separation.—Local Self-government.—The Mad Rush.—A Long Journey.—The Land of Promise.—The Return 153

CHAPTER XVIII.

QUEENSLAND (continued).

Looking a-head.—A Pleasant Life.—Amateur Squatting.—Unfulfilled Hopes.—The Mad Season.—Good Times.—Want of Labour.—An Emigration Lecturer.—A Pleasant Future.—The Right and Wrong Emigrants.—Failure and Success.—Revival and Work.—The Future of Queensland 167

CONTENTS.

CHAPTER XIX.

[illegible] ... 176

CHAPTER XX.
QUEENSLAND (*continued*).

... 184

CHAPTER XXI.
QUEENSLAND (*continued*).

... 193

CHAPTER XXII.
NORTHERN AUSTRALIA.

...

CHAPTER XXIII.
NORTHERN AUSTRALIA (*continued*).

...

CHAPTER XXIV.
SOUTH AUSTRALIA, WESTERN AUSTRALIA, AND TASMANIA.

...

LIST OF ENGRAVINGS TO VOL. II.

Near Newcastle, on the Hunter, New South Wales . . . *To face page*	126
Harper's Hill, Hunter River	128
Port Stephens	129
On the Cow Pasture River	133
The Hawkesbury, New South Wales . .	134
Falls of the Weather-board . . .	136
Cockatoo Island	137
Goat Island . .	138
Australian Aboriginals fishing .	143
View near Botany Bay .	143
Mount Kiera, New South Wales .	146
Tom Thumb's Lagoon, New South Wales .	149
Gully at Woolongong . .	150
Lake Illawarra, New South Wales .	151
Twofold Bay . . .	153
Fairy Lake, New South Wales .	154
Map of Queensland . .	158
Native Encampment .	164
Return of Burke and Wills to Cooper's Creek .	182
Kangaroo Point, Brisbane (from Bowen Terrace) .	187
Brisbane (from South Brisbane) . .	188
The Boabab-Tree . .	190
Gladstone, Queensland .	203
New Zealand Gully near Rockhampton, Queensland .	205
Baines River, Northern Australia . .	207
Stampede of Pack Horses (Northern Territory) .	208
Natives of Carpentaria .	209
Townsville, Queensland .	210
The Burra Burra Copper Mines . .	211

LIST OF ENGRAVINGS

	To face page
MAP OF THE SETTLED PORTIONS OF SOUTH AUSTRALIA	212
ADELAIDE FROM THE RIVER TORRENS	213
GOVERNMENT HOUSE, ADELAIDE	214
LYNDOCH AND ADELAIDE HARBOUR	215
WATERFALL NEAR ADELAIDE	216
PORT LINCOLN, SOUTH AUSTRALIA	217
PERTH, TASMANIA	218
HOBART TOWN, TASMANIA	219
THE QUEEN, HOBART TOWN	220
SOURCE OF THE DERWENT, TASMANIA	221
THE DERWENT	222
BLACK MAN'S COVE, TASMANIA	223
MARIA ISLAND, TASMANIA	224
LAUNCESTON, TASMANIA	225
LAUNCESTON, TASMANIA	226
TASMAN'S ISLAND	227
CATARACT GLEN, MOUNT WELLINGTON, TASMANIA	228
PORT ARTHUR, TASMANIA	229
LAKE ST. CLAIR, TASMANIA	230
BANKS OF THE PLENTY, TASMANIA	231

followed Hume and Hovill; they discovered more practicable routes and other country; but to Hume, who was a Sydney native—his father being an Irish Presbyterian clergyman—and to Hovill, an old sailor, belongs the credit and honour of teaching the world that rivers, and important ones, existed in the heart of Australia.

So soon as the Murrumbidgee leaves the higher mountains that are the cradle of its infant, though turbulent, waters, it passes through a country of exceeding beauty and of great richness. Every here and there along its banks patches of agricultural land are met with, and picturesque and prosperous settlements are to be found nestling under the hills that sometimes rise sheer up the valleys with a clean sweep of a thousand feet, whilst oftener still they are terraced from point to point, but always pleasant to look upon. The river itself is bright and clear, the air so sweet and fresh that it is a joy simply to live in such a climate. Game and wild fowl are plentiful, the trees and flowers and shrubs of exceeding beauty, and all the natural surroundings of the place of a character admirably adapted for the pleasure and comfort of man.

CHAPTER XIV.

NEW SOUTH WALES (*continued*).

THE RIVER HUNTER.—NEWCASTLE.—THE TOWNS UP THE RIVER.—A NEW INDUSTRY. — RAILWAY EXTENSION. — THE MACLEAY RIVER. — THE CLARENCE.—THE RICHMOND.—THE FAR NORTH OF NEW SOUTH WALES.

THE most interesting and **characteristic features of** New South Wales— with the exception of the **known portions of the Blue** Mountains—are **to be found** upon the coast and the country lying between it and the mountain **ranges.** Whilst Port Jackson stands foremost in importance, and, indeed, in **point of beauty, there are** many other places on the seaboard well worthy of **attention and description.** First among these—in commercial importance, **at any rate—is the river** Hunter and the **town of** Newcastle, some fifty or sixty miles to the north of Sydney. **The natives** used to call the waters upon the banks of which Newcastle is situate, Mulubindi; the early settlers, with that spirit of loyalty with which they are so strongly actuated, changed the soft liquids of the black fellow into the loud and emphatic-sounding Kingston.

Before the years of the present century had commenced, a cast-away boat's crew found masses of coal lying strewn upon the beach away north of the debouchment of the waters of the river. This discovery indeed prospecting. Seams of coal were soon discovered. Coal River was the name given to the stream, and that of Newcastle to the settlement made upon its bank. The river had, however, been called the Hunter on the occasion of its discovery in 1797, and that name it retains to the present. It rises in the Liverpool ranges, and is fed by several heads, all of them flowing through picturesque valleys. It has a length of two hundred miles, chiefly in a south-easterly direction towards the sea. Its lower course is through a rich agricultural country, for the most part low-lying and subject to inundation.

Newcastle is pleasantly situate on a gently-rising hill, and on the ridge by which it is capped, on the south bank of the Hunter. Below the town, and at the mouth of the river, there used to be an island (Noddy's Island, it was called, and strange stories of a convict who resided there are told), now connected with the mainland by means of a breakwater, of considerable use and value to the shipping visiting the harbour. Some idea of the importance of the shipping interest of Newcastle may be gathered from the fact, that nearly eight hundred thousand tons of coal are annually shipped from the port. In a very few years there is little doubt but European exports will be made direct to Newcastle, instead of having to undergo all the charges and cost consequent upon re-shipment at Melbourne or Sydney.

To the geologist the neighbourhood of the Hunter is of surpassing interest. Ferns of exceeding beauty are found throughout the entire measure of the coal beds, and specimens of fossil flora are to be met with in every direction; and although marine fossils are rare, they are only sufficiently so to make the search for them a pleasant one.

There are several prosperous towns and villages at distances varying from ten to twenty miles from Newcastle. Hexham, equi-distant from Newcastle and Maitland, is one of the most important of these. The surrounding country is flat and swampy, but very much of it of unusual richness. The river hereabouts has its course broken by queerly-shaped islands, upon several of which oranges of capital quality are grown. The country is also famous for its crops of maize and other cereals. The towns of Maitland, East and West, are both of them important places, surrounded by a rich agricultural country. The two towns are situate on the banks of a tributary of the Hunter, Wallis's Creek, and not far from the meeting of their waters. Although the land in the immediate neighbourhood of the towns is flat, there are some picturesque hills

SCENE ON THE HUNTER, NEW SOUTH WALES.

at a little distance, from the sides of which the floods of winter rush upon the plain below, giving it the appearance of an inland sea. These floods occasionally do damage; but they are also the cause of the richness of the soil. The quality of the deep black loam held by the farmers of the district may be judged from the fact that it is no unusual thing to cut half-a-dozen heavy crops of lucern from the same ground in the course of a year, and this for a long series of years.

East Maitland was the first laid out township of the name. The site chosen was a pleasant, but in almost every other respect an unsuitable one, and nearly all the material prosperity of the place is centred at West Maitland, about a mile and a-half away. Here there are flour-mills, tobacco manufactories, numerous large business establishments, and public buildings, the original town, however, retaining the public offices and the assizes of the district. It boasts also of one of the best horse and cattle markets of New **South Wales.** East Maitland on horse-sale day is a scene of great bustle and excitement of a thoroughly Australian character. Breeders and buyers meet together and make as motley a group, as full of life and spirits, as keen and shrewd, as any similar gathering in Yorkshire could furnish.

One of the most interesting industries of New South Wales has been established at the village of Waratah, about four miles to the north of Newcastle. The manufacture of a common kind of pottery has been carried on for some time, and, from the quality of the clay discovered, great things are expected, when skilled labour is brought to bear upon the industry. This is one of the many openings that exist, in plenty, all over Australia for men with technical knowledge and means to develop the resources of the country. One other of the products of the Hunter River has recently been utilised, **and** promises to lead to the establishment of a valuable field of labour. Reference has already been made to the crops of maize grown at various points on **the** river. No ordinary field of Indian corn would give an adequate idea of the exceeding richness of some of the forests—for forests they are—of standing grain to be seen hereabouts. The plants rise up straight and strong, and stand, some of them, eight feet high. For many years the cobs were gathered, and the immense mass of green stalk that supported them left to cumber the ground. Sometimes they were thrown to the cattle, often they were burned, and generally they were looked upon as a nuisance. Lately, however, an attempt to turn this mass of matter into money has been made, and the attempt promises to be successful.

The high price of paper in **the colony, and the scarcity of paper-making** material in Europe, led people to think of the great waste of fibre consequent upon the ordinary method of dealing with the maize stalks. Several attempts at paper-making from maize fibre were made in the colony, but the high wages rate and the want of proper appliances **prevented the** experiment being carried out to any very great extent. This partial failure had, however, one happy effect. The freight charges upon so light a material as is the maize fibre, made it almost impossible to export it in its natural state, or at any rate to do so with a profit. The idea of reducing it to pulp, drying it, and then by hydraulic pressure bringing it within convenient limits, was acted upon, and with considerable success. When cleaned and dried and pressed, the fibre can be shipped at the lowest possible rate of freight for dead weight. Indeed, so far as the material itself is concerned and its safety on the voyage, it might almost be shipped as ballast, for no amount of ill-usage, short of actual saturation with water, could have any appreciable effect upon its quality or condition. It packs as tight and lies as close as so many blocks of granite; yet, **on being** subjected to a proper and very simple process, it becomes a pulp **adapted in** every way to the purposes of the paper-maker. After a few years paper-**making** will doubtless be one of the established industries of the Hunter, and in the meantime the export of the compressed pulp **adds to** the material advantages of the district.

Among the other things that tend to increase the importance of Newcastle may be reckoned the Great Northern Railway, the starting-point of which is fixed at the coal-port of the north. The first part of the course of the railway is through and by the coal-fields of the district, and at the same time it is, throughout nearly the whole of its completed course, in close proximity to the rich agricultural districts already referred to. Passing the Maitlands, the line proceeds on to Singleton, a town about half-way between West Maitland and Musswellbrook. After running up the valley of the river for about eighty miles, the railway is carried over it at Singleton by means of a bridge, built at a cost of some £50,000.

Save that it is a town of considerable importance on a line of railway, and that it has always been a roadside town ever since its establishment, there is little specially noticeable about Singleton. Among its public institutions there may be noticed a public hospital and the mechanics' institute. Both of these are liberally supported, and fulfil the work for which they are intended. Patrick Plains surround the town, and present as pleasant and prosperous a scene as need be looked upon. A great deal of the land is taken up for dairy-farming, and by-and-by the export of Patrick Plains butter to England may

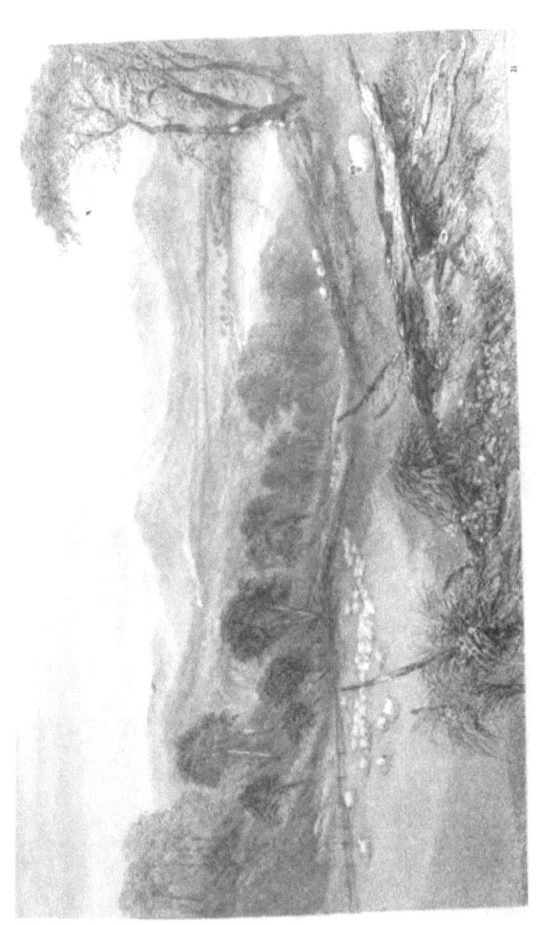

fairly be looked for. The plains are well watered by tributaries of the
Hunter, and upon every creek, under pleasantly placed clumps of trees, and,
indeed, in every direction, comfortable homesteads are to be found.

From Singleton the Great Northern Railway runs on to Muswellbrook, the
country retaining its appearance of quiet, homely comfort the whole way.
At Aberdeen the line is again carried across the river by means of a substantial bridge. By the time the railway reaches Aberdeen the character of
the country changes. Instead of the long level plains, the rich river banks,
and deep beds of loam, mountains and hills combine to give a character to the
scene. From Aberdeen the railway will be carried on to Murrundi; and
although the country through which it will pass is mountainous, many parts
of it are admirably adapted for cultivation, and it is tolerably well settled.

Two years after the opening of the line to Muswellbrook, the extension to
Scone was, on the 18th April, 1871, formally opened by Lord Belmore, the
governor of the colony. This extension not only opens up a considerable
extent of coal-bearing country, but places the agriculturists of the Kingdon
Ponds Plain within cheap and easy communication of the markets of Newcastle and Sydney.

Port Stephens is about twenty miles north of the mouth of the Hunter,
and as a harbour, although never utilised, save as a place of refuge, is
infinitely preferable to the latter. The Myall River runs parallel with the
coast, and connects Port Stephens with a salt-water lake, also called Myall.
Stroud, a town chiefly dependent on the timber of the district, is not far away
inland. Gloucester, a small place in the middle of a rugged county, is about
thirty miles farther inland, and is the chief town—indeed, almost the only
one—of a county of the same name. Running up the coast still farther north
the Manning River is next met with. This stream discharges itself into the
Pacific by two mouths. It flows through a well-wooded country, and during
its course receives many tributary streams. Although the mountains pre-
dominate, there are many large patches of good agricultural land, and settlement is everywhere met with, whilst industrial pursuits of various kinds are
numerous. Port Macquarie is the next point of importance on the coast, and
to this succeeds the Macleay River. This latter is a magnificent stream,
draining an area of nearly 5000 square miles, large portions of which are of
an exceedingly valuable character. The Macleay has a course of 200 miles
through country thickly timbered with cedar and other valuable trees. On
its banks are two or three small towns, and at short intervals agricultural
settlement has taken place. Kempsey, East and West, are the chief of the

L L

Macleay River towns; but neither of them are of any very great importance. The sugar-cane has been profitably grown on the banks of the Macleay, and heavy **crops** of maize are common. The mountains are lofty and the **scenery wild; but** alluvial flats are plentiful and easily brought **under** cultivation. In some places the ridges of rocks run straight out from the mountains and close in the banks of the river, forming ravines and chasms of an extraordinary and wild beauty. Strange flowers abound, and flowering shrubs grow out of the fissures of the rocks that overhang the water.

After the Macleay comes the Clarence, a still more important stream, draining an area of 8,000 square miles, and running a course nearly 250 miles long. The Clarence empties into the Pacific about 400 miles north of Sydney. For nearly 70 miles above its mouth it has an average breadth of nearly half a mile. Near and around its head-waters and its tributary streams, rich mineral deposits have been discovered, and several gold-fields worked. Grafton, the principal town of the river, is situate about fifty miles up the stream, which is navigable for 30 miles beyond this point. Ships drawing ten feet of water have no difficulty in getting up to Grafton, and from the port a very large portion **of** the produce of an exceedingly rich pastoral, agricultural, and mining district is conveyed to the seaboard and to the neighbouring colonies. Nearly all the settlement is on the banks of the river and in the valleys running down from a not very elevated range of hills a little distance away. A low-lying and isolated series of hills, called the Coal Range, runs in an easterly and westerly direction, some miles to the north of Grafton, and the only roads from Tenterfield to the latter township are through the gaps of these mountains. As may be understood from the name, coal, though not in very considerable quantities, has been found in the hills. The plentiful supply of firewood everywhere to be met with has had the effect of directing attention from the coal deposits of the district.

A long-stretching, low, sandy, and scrub-covered coast leads from the mouth of the Clarence to the Richmond River, distant thirty miles, or thereabouts, farther north. Here and there a ridge of sandstone breaks the tiring monotony of the scene, and in some places signs of settlement are met with; but, on the whole, this part of the Australian coast presents a melancholy view to the travellers along the coast by sea. Sometimes the blue ridges of the Dividing Range may be seen, but the distance is too great for any of their features to be distinctly recognised. Here and there a trifling indentation in the land gives variety to the view, but in no instance does it rise above the most ordinary appearance of a low-lying sea-coast.

The traveller who makes the journey ashore, parallel with and a few miles from the coast, although he would have more difficulties to encounter than the sea voyager, would meet with objects of far more interest. The swamps and lagoons, round which he would have to make his way, have upon their borders vegetation so luxuriant that the term sub-tropical may with all propriety be applied to it. Strange birds and stranger flowers continually present themselves. Whenever the ground rises from the ordinary level of the country, objects of interest increase in number, the waters of the creeks flow over, if not golden sands, strange pebbles, and by basalts carpeted with flowers, having perfumes as sweet and colours as bright as the world can show. The birds build their nests after fashions that would seem to indicate a knowledge of a want of necessity on their parts of conforming to the ordinary routine of the bird world in other places; their eggs are more strangely marked and coloured than elsewhere, the slenderest stem serves for a lodging place, and the nest itself is of the most frail character possible. Lizards that shimmer and shine with a thousand rays of purple and gold run up and across the paths, wholly heedless of man, whilst the long dull-looking iguana hangs from the bark of trees and stares through vacancy at a world of which the traveller knows not, but upon the residents in which the strange creature lives and enjoys himself.

The Richmond River is the highest important stream on the east coast of Australia within the boundaries of New South Wales. It rises on Mount Lindsey, the highest point of the Macpherson Range. These ranges form not only the geographical but a natural boundary between the colonies of New South Wales and Queensland. At the mouth of the Richmond is situate the town of Ballina. There are other towns on and in the neighbourhood of the river, but none of them of any importance. The entrance to the Richmond is bounded on the north by a bluff headland that stands out bold and well defined, and contrasts strongly with the low coast-land to the south. Soon after passing the Richmond River the hills of the Dividing Range close in upon the coast, and when the boundary of Queensland is crossed the country by the sea-side assumes a much more defined and characteristic appearance. The Tweed is the last stream within the New South Wales borders, but in consequence of its mouth being blocked by a sand-bar, it is of little use in a commercial point of view. Point Danger marks the division of the colonies on the coast, and immediately to the south of it is the entrance to the Tweed. Point Danger runs out boldly into the sea, and is a well-known landmark. The land on either side of it is low, but shoreward the mountains

AUSTRALIA ILLUSTRATED.

rise and run for a considerable distance to the west, and then join the main Dividing Range of the continent.

The belt of country lying between the Blue Mountains and the sea, and extending northwards from Port Jackson for nearly 400 **miles** to Point Danger, has, with few exceptions, been settled within the last twenty-two years. The earlier settlements were nearly all to the west and south-west of Sydney, and consequently contain some of the most beautiful scenery of the whole country, as well as some of the most extensive and cultivated districts.

CHAPTER XV.

NEW SOUTH WALES (continued).

THE FIRST EXPLORERS.—THE COW PASTURE.—THE HAWKESBURY.—EARLY RUMOURS OF GOLD.—OVERLAND TO CHINA.—THE WESTERN RAILWAY.—THE PARAMATTA RIVER.—THE WATERFALLS.—BATHURST.

The mountains running parallel to the coast—the Blue Mountains, for a coast and main ranges were at first indiscriminately called—had an intense and abiding interest for the early visitors to the eastern shores of the continent of Australia. Their long-spreading and dim, mysterious outline ever attracted attention, and appeared to exact enquiry. Cook and his companions, as they sailed slowly towards the north, must sometimes have caught glimpses of the almost level line of cobalt that the clearness of the atmosphere would now and then reveal. On the days when the sun went down with a clearer light than usual, a varying mist of delicate colouring caused by the moving of the mists upon the mountains or the waving of the treetops upon the far-off ridges, would add another charm to the scene, and increase the wonder of the spectator. To the first settlers the mountains possessed an indescribable charm. In the very earliest days plans for penetrating into and crossing over them were formed and attempted. The first records of the settlement tell **of adventure** and suffering in connection with these attempts. Singularly enough, a search for gold was connected with the earliest endeavour to cross the hills. A party of convicts, twenty in number, got an idea into their heads that China lay on the other side of the mountains, and that in China gold could be obtained in plenty. They had laid their plans with tolerable

THE COW PASTURES, NEW SOUTH WALES.

wisdom, and are supposed to have penetrated pretty far into the coast **range.** The character of the country, however, and the impossibility of recruiting their soon-exhausted stock of provisions, had the effect of making them return towards the settlement at Paramatta. They were captured by the officials, and severely punished; but it was a good many years before the belief, that **over** the **mountains** lay China and inexhaustible gold-fields, died out.

Of **the** newcomers, however, **men were not the** first to explore **the** country to the west of Sydney. Soon after the settlement of Port Jackson a couple of bulls and five cows strayed away, and were not discovered **for** several years afterwards, and then they had increased to **a** herd **sixty or** seventy in number. Led by a wise instinct, these cattle had forsaken the comparatively spare pastures around Sydney, followed up the rivers and water-courses, until practicable crossing-places were reached, and then settled down in the rich pastures beyond. So wise did these natives of the Cape of Good Hope prove themselves in their selections of a locality, that the place—the Cow Pasture it has been called ever since—is to this day one of the richest and most prosperous agricultural districts of New South Wales. In some portions of the district there is a perfect network of rivers, and the scenery is of exceeding beauty. The views on the Warragamba, the Nepean, the Hawkesbury, and the Cow Pasture Rivers, afford lively and accurate ideas of some of the most beautiful places in and around the course of the streams named. These rivers, as well as many other tributary streams of minor importance, all join together to form the Hawkesbury. It would be difficult to conceive scenery more beautiful than that which characterises the junction of the Nepean with the latter river. The Blue Mountains close in upon the rivers, whilst the latter winds round all the points and corners as though loth to leave places so pleasant. This serpentine peculiarity characterises the Hawkesbury for the greater part of its course. For every mile of country it crosses, it encircles three or four, and thus fertilises a wide stretch of country. In common with most of the Australian rivers, the Hawkesbury is liable to heavy floods. It is recorded that on one occasion its waters rose fully a hundred feet above their ordinary level, and great was the destruction in consequence. When the storm rages up in the mountains, the torrents descend with a marvellous force, and pouring their waters together in the valleys below, makes an inland sea of what had been the day before a picture of prosperous contentment. These floods have had the effect of driving settlement somewhat back from the banks of the river, and several prosperous places are established a few miles away from the Hawkesbury, and on both banks important towns abound, and, indeed, throughout the whole of what may be fairly termed the Riverine district east of the Blue Mountains.

Having in view the subsequent discovery of gold and its influence on the colony, it is not a little interesting to read of the earliest rumours with reference to it. In the last year of the eighteenth century, the then infant colony was thrown into a state of excitement by a discovery of gold alleged to have been made by a convict. This prisoner declared that he had discovered a gold mine somewhere on the banks of the bay between Sydney Cove and the Heads of Port Jackson. So circumstantial and elaborate was he in his description of his proceedings and the locality of the gold, that the Government on two occasions organised parties of workers, who were placed under the guidance of the pretended discoverer. On the first occasion he managed to leave the party in the bush, and returned alone to Sydney. Of course he was severely punished, but still persisted in his statement with reference to the existence of the treasure, and showed the governor specimens of the ore he professed to have obtained. On the strength of this, a second party was despatched, but so strict a watch was kept upon the movements of the discoverer, that, after several ineffectual attempts to escape, he acknowledged that he had practised an imposture for the purpose of getting on board a vessel then on the point of returning to Europe. The gold dust he said he had manufactured by filing down a guinea and a brass button. Notwithstanding this imposture, the belief in the existence of gold was never abandoned, and indeed the auriferous character of the country was perfectly well known to the governing classes from the earliest days of exploration; but the desirability of making the fact known, was never recognised. The character of the majority of the people supplied a sufficient reason for this reticence.

The search for gold, however, had little to do with the opening up of the country. The settlement of the districts selected by the strayed cattle proceeded rapidly, and as the natural riches of the country became developed, the desire to cross over the mountains became intensified, and every year brought its story of some new enterprise. By the middle of 1789, the Hawkesbury had been traced to its source in the mountains, and the wild character of the country had the effect of retarding the work of explory for a time. A regularly organised party attempted to penetrate within the hills in the December of that year, but its members never got within a dozen miles of the base of the mountains, and they returned to the settlement after an absence *of* some nine or ten days. Private enterprise, however, never failed. Some of the Irish convicts, struck with the resemblance between the Blue Mountains **and** the green hills of their native **land,** started on a journey towards **home.** That they **were** fully impressed **with** the truth of the thing they hoped for, may be gathered from the fact that one of these private expeditions was detained for a considerable time because of the inability of the party to obtain possession **of a compass.** Once possessed of this, they were sure, they said, by keeping a due west course, to make their home. They obtained a compass at last, or rather they stole from a book the points of the compass printed on paper, and with this blind guide they started. Many **of** them were never heard of again. For years after, wandering bushmen would occasionally come across a skeleton that told too well of the fate of many of those **who first attempted the** passage of the Blue Mountains. The sufferings of **some of these** poor wanderers must have been intense. Of one party, some **three or** four were, after long searching for, recovered, who had existed on grass for five days. The overland journey to China has already been alluded to. A story is told of one who joined in that expedition, who, after wandering in the bush for several days, came upon a hut in which there resided a woman of his acquaintance, and of whom he gravely asked how she had managed to get to China before him? The poor fellow was within ten miles of his starting-point, and had been walking in a circle for several days. The same peculiar mode of travelling often attaches itself to people lost in the bush to this time.

Thus the first score years of the present century passed away without any very great progress being made in the way of Australian discovery. Now and then a party was organised by the Government, but the result of their labours was generally very small. The love of adventure and private enterprise at length succeeded, but only after repeated trials and sore defeats. Time after time had the mountains been attacked, but they always repelled the invader. Deep gorges were discovered, but only to show the discoverers that **the** only way out was the narrow valley by which they had obtained an entrance. Sometimes the sheer upright wall of a precipice would bar the way, and oftener still the ridges of the mountain-sides threatened with destruction those who trod upon the crumbling rock with which its edges were fringed. Deep dark valleys stretched away into impenetrable obscurity. In some places the forest trees grew so closely together that the light of day rarely penetrated to the ground from which they sprung. Dense jungles barred the way, and mountain torrents forbad further progress. Here and there a level plain would tempt the wanderer, by promise of pleasant places, into jungles more dense, to the banks of rivers more rapid, by the side of steeper mountains, such as rugged rock-strewn hillsides, than he had met with before, and drive him back to seek less promising though more practicable routes. Disappointment, death sometimes, suffering always, attended these attempts; but failure ever led to renewed endeavour, and at length the labours of the big-hearted men of the old days were rewarded. The "heaven seeking" barriers were overtopped; rivers, whose waters were gathered up in mountain gorges of which the world had never known, were followed up and crossed; narrow ridges of rock, both sides of which ran down for hundreds of feet before they found the broken surface of the vales below, were traversed; in some instances half a score of miles had to be travelled over before a single mile of real progress was made; pleasant glens were discovered and dry patches painfully plodded over, before the last important resting-place on the journey over the hills was reached. The goal was worthy of all the pain and trouble it had cost, and the journeyers were content.

Wentworth, Blaxland, and Lawson—names to be ever remembered by Australians—crossed the mountains in the May and June of 1813. So modest were these men that only the latest record of their labours has been published. The dangers and perils are all left unspoken of. The world has only been told that one morning in the July of the year named, these brave men passed over the highest ridge of the Blue Mountains, and pointed out the track to a new and richer Australia beyond. The western watershed of the colony was, however, not reached by them. They traced up the eastern running streams until they came into a country the wild and picturesque character of which is admirably depicted in the sketch of the Falls of the Weatherboard and Jamison's Valley. The rocks over which the water falls are fully 3,000 feet above the waters of the Pacific that break upon the beach less than fifty miles away. There is a marvellous beauty surrounding this resting-place. On either side, in one of the passes through the mountains, the rocks rise straight up for nearly 800 feet. Not very far from the Falls of the Weatherboard is the Vale of Clwyd, a place of special loveliness, in the midst of a country that may challenge comparison with any mountain scenery in the world. Of the Valley of the Weatherboard itself, Darwin the naturalist says: "An immense gulf opens through the trees which border the path at a depth of perhaps 1,500 feet. Walking on a few yards one stands on the brink of a vast precipice, and below one sees a grand bay or gulf—for I know not what other name to give it—thickly

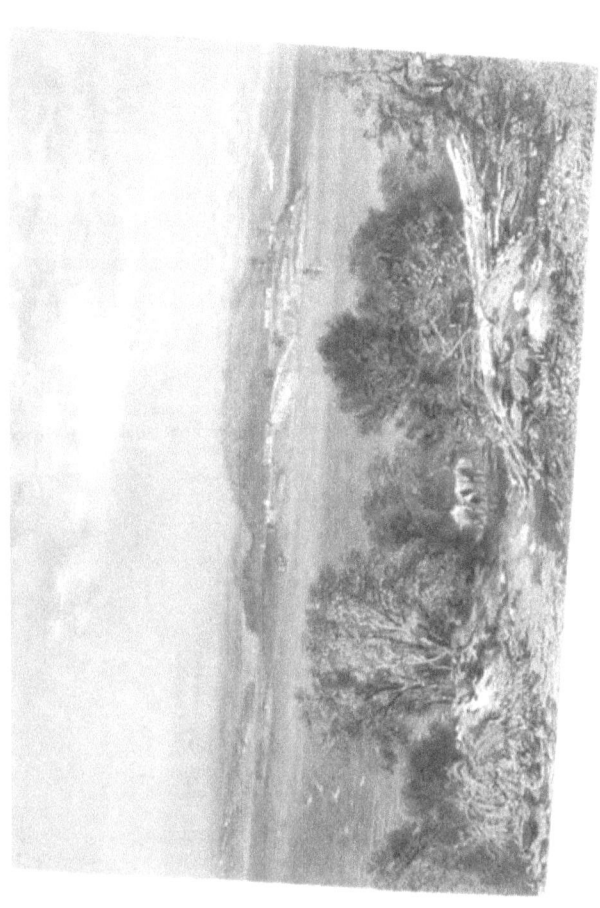

covered with forest. The point of view is situate as if at the head of a bay, the line of cliff diverging on each side, and showing on each side headland behind headland, as in a low sea-coast. The cliffs are so absolutely vertical that in many places a person standing on the edge and throwing down a stone can see it strike the trees in the abyss below."

Want of provisions, rather than a full satisfaction at the result of their journey, caused Wentworth and his companions to retrace their steps after having travelled so far into the hills. Their report of the country they had discovered had the effect of expediting the work of exploration considerably. The Government at once organised a party for the purpose of continuing the work from the point at which the pioneer explorers had ended their western journey. Within a month the last of the ranges of the Blue Mountains were crossed, and the far-spreading plains of Bathurst reached. It was like the discovery of a new world. All that the Australia of the coast lacked—broad pastures—were here in plenty. Within two years of the discovery a road had been made over the mountains, and cattle in hundreds and thousands were taken into the new territory. Every year added fresh discoveries to the list of those already made, until at last the great discovery of all, that of "Australia Felix," closed the work for a time.

The Blue Mountains, as is the fashion with most mountains, remain pretty much as they were when first crossed. The means and mode of crossing them is, however, very much altered. Now, instead of a track winding round and over and across the ridges, the reefs, and the valleys, a railway spans the vales, pierces the mountains, and accomplishes in a few hours the journey that once occupied weeks and months. One peculiarity of this, one of the most wonderful railways in the world, is especially worthy of notice. Its rails have been laid down, its roadway formed, and the journey from Sydney to the West made, as nearly as possible upon and along the track pursued by the explorers of 1813. This track followed a native trail, the convict-made road followed the track, and now the railway crosses the mountains on the same line. No better route, indeed no other practicable one, has been discovered, and the engineer of to-day has been content and glad to follow the footsteps of the Australian savage of ages ago.

The Western Railway of New South Wales is not only interesting as a monument of engineering skill, but because of the country it passes through and opens up; but by far the best view of the country for the first twenty miles or so is by way of the Paramatta River. Immediately after leaving Sydney, Goat Island is passed, and a couple of miles further up, Cockatoo Island.

Both of these islands are simple sandstone hills rising out of the water. Goat Island is used as a powder magazine, and Cockatoo as a convict settlement. They each contain immense chambers excavated from the solid rock, which are perhaps the best specimens of that sort of troglodyte description of dwelling-place in the world. As the stream is followed up, the banks narrow in, the passage is made through orange groves, and the scene becomes one of exceeding beauty. The country was originally of a wild and rugged character; but the pleasant-looking houses, with their surrounding orange groves descending in terraces to the banks of the river, the quaintly arranged gardens, and the islands that here and there dot the waterway, take all characteristics of wildness away from the scene.

The town of Parramatta stands at the bend of the river, and has always been a place of considerable importance. The first governor of the colony selected it as the vice-regal place of residence, and, under the name of Rose Hill, it was once the one aristocratic settlement in the colony. It is now a flourishing town, having several extensive manufactories—in one of which Sydney tweed, a cloth of excellent quality, and having a high reputation, is made. Churches, schools, and kindred public institutions abound. The population numbers between 6,000 and 7,000.

Travelling west, the first place of importance arrived at is Penrith, a small town situate on the River Nepean, and surrounded by country of the character indicated in the sketches of the Cow Pasture, Fairlight Glen, and the Hawkesbury. After passing Penrith, the orange groves, that have hitherto given so much of character to the country, are lost sight of, and their place taken by high ranges and turbulent watercourses. Here and there a valley has been cultivated; but these occur at rare intervals, nor is a settlement of this kind likely to be very much added to. The railway is carried over the River Nepean at Penrith by means of a viaduct, that stands out in strange contrast with the wild country around. As an example of what has been done in New South Wales in the matter of engineering, it may be stated that this viaduct has three openings each 186 feet wide. The bridge proper—that is, the stone arches independent of the approaches—is over 600 feet long. The whole is constructed of solid masonry, and would be esteemed a creditable piece of engineering work in any part of the world.

West of the Nepean, the Blue Mountains, as distinguished from the Coast Range, rise up in vast irregular masses. Across and alongside the defiles of the hills the railway is conducted by a zigzag, or rather a series of zigzags. At the end of each section of the zigzag the trains are run on to a level

GOAT ISLAND.

twists of the rivers are one by one being taken advantage of. Flats are flooded by means of diverted water-courses. Hill-sides are irrigated, vineyards formed upon them, orchards planted and gardens tended, and all with a pleasant and a profitable reward. Day by day and year after year these influences are brought to bear upon lands hitherto esteemed worthless, and always with the happiest results. Comfort and contentment reign, and a prosperous future seems assured for this new and peaceful "City of the Plain." Of the far-spreading plains beyond, their deep mysterious dales, their solitary clumps of trees, the men who have perished in the passing over them, the varied tortured forms of life, the strange mysteries with which their out-of-the-way corners are invested, all the thousand and one strange varieties of life with which they abound, and of the long unrecorded list of wonders by which they are surrounded, little can be said here; but, in the time to come, many volumes will be written, and then the list will be incomplete. New phases of life are every day being discovered, and fresh applications of the good things that providence is constantly revealing are being made. Every newly-found water-course leads to new homes being formed, and every experiment in home-making tends to enrich the country and its people.

CHAPTER XVI.

NEW SOUTH WALES (*concluded*).

SOUTH OF SYDNEY.—CHARACTER OF COUNTRY AND PEOPLE.—VARIED EMPLOYMENTS. — FISHING. — RANDWICK.—ILLAWARRA.—FOREST TREES.—WOLLONGONG.—SHOALHAVEN.—ULLADULLA.—THE RHOMBOID OF MONARO.

THE coast of Australia—from the heads of Port Jackson to Cape Howe, as well as the districts lying between the coast and the Coast Range, and in the valleys between the latter and the Blue Mountains—possesses many points of extreme interest. So old are some of the settlements of the district, that the term primitive may with perfect propriety be applied to them. All up and down the line of country referred to, in secluded valleys, and on sunny hill-sides, queer, quaint, old-fashioned settlements and villages are to be met with, and the inhabitants are in their manners and customs just as retiring and simple as the places in which they live. Places and people alike are

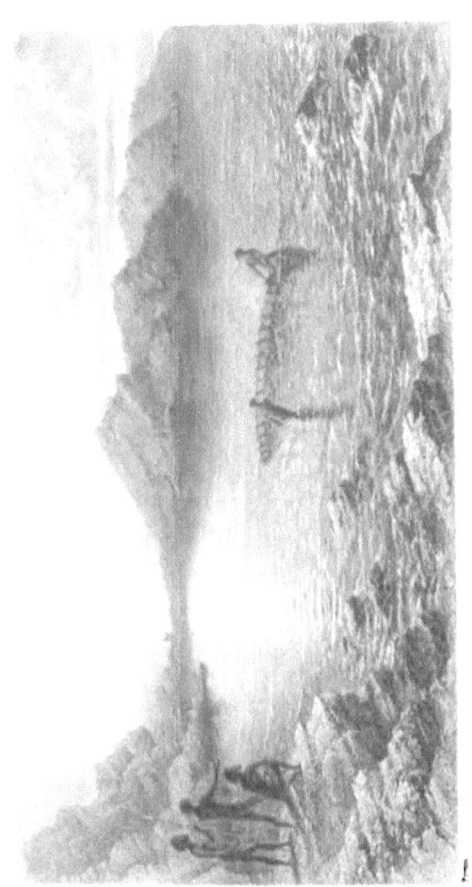

wonderfully "old-fashioned," and present as **few of** the ordinarily accepted features of colonists and of colonial settlements **as** can well be imagined. Here may be found

> "The sheltered cot, the cultivated farm,
> The never-failing brook, the busy mill,
> The decent church,"

and all the surroundings of a thoroughly comfortable country life. The employments of the people are of a strangely mixed character. The farmer of to-day may be the fisherman of to-morrow, the gold-miner of next week, or the bushman of all the "unconsidered trifles" of time, of which less primitive people take so little account. The ocean that breaks upon the east coast of Australia, rolls with a long continued sweep—unbroken, indeed, save by the narrow strip of disjointed land called New Zealand—from the shores of the "golden South America," and bears to the Australian settler treasure in plenty. Thus the farmer-miner-bushman takes to the sea, and levies contributions, sometimes upon the leviathans thereof, but oftener still upon the uncountable shoals of fish that sweep down by the coast and into the straits below. This source of wealth is, however, too much neglected, yet, there are few of the "undeveloped resources" of Australia so worthy of the attention of the settler as are the various fishing banks with which the coast abounds. Hitherto this kind of wealth has been almost entirely overlooked, or so little attended to as to be scarcely worth noticing. At some points on the coast parties of Chinese have engaged in fishing and the curing of fish, but their mode of dealing with the produce of their labour fails to commend it **to** the **tastes of** white people, hence their operations have been on a very limited scale. There are, however, attempts made to supply Sydney and such up-country towns as are accessible by rail, with fish. How inadequate these attempts are may be gathered from the fact that in 1870 the entire supply was estimated at about 50,000 bushels of fish taken by net, and about 5,000 dozen of fish—averaging about seventy-two pounds to the dozen—taken by line. This would give an average of about one ounce of fish per week to every probable consumer. The mode of distributing the fish to the customer is even more objectionable than the limited manner in which the fishing is conducted; and in both these directions there is ample **scope for the growth of a large** and profitable industry. It is not merely that a large consumption **of fresh** fish would result from the adoption of a systematic mode of supply—there are large numbers of fish common to the southern and eastern coasts of Australia admirably adapted for preservation by means of salting, smoking, **and otherwise;** and for this description of food large sums **of money are annually sent out** of the colony. The mullet of Lake Macquarie, when properly cured **and** smoked, is little if at all inferior to **a** genuine Finnan haddie," and infinitely better than the so-called haddock with which the ordinary Londoner is **content.** The " Moruya Nonn gai " **is** better still, and need not fear comparison with any smoked fish in the world. The king-fish, though by no means so good as either of the other two named, is infinitely superior to the ling and cod, imported from Europe and America, whilst the barracoota, the schnapper, the whiting, and the gartish **are** all excellent, and admirably adapted for food whether in a fresh or cured state.

Now the whole of the six hundred miles of the **coast** of New South Wales has every here and there stations admirably adapted for the spawning, feeding, and taking of the kinds named, besides many others. The bays at **the** mouths of the several rivers are equally well adapted for the preservation **of** the young **fry.** Without any process of preservation the supply is inexhaustible, **and it is not** unusual for the fishers of Port Jackson—or rather of the waters outside the heads—to discontinue their labours, not because fish **fail them, but** that it is deemed unadvisable to glut the market. All the bays on the coast abound with fish of, for the most part, the most delicious description, and it is to be hoped that very soon the attention of some of the fishermen of Great Britain may be turned towards the systematic working of these treasure grounds. One other fish remains to be noticed. The rock oyster of Sydney is as fine a flavoured bivalve as the most famous native of the English coast, and its preservation is worthy of all the care and attention that can be given to it.

There are fields of waving corn to be reaped as well as the treasures of the waves to gather, **and** they repeat upon a smaller scale the ever-varying beauty **of the sea by which they** are bounded. Quietly and calmly as the great ocean waves roll **in towards the** shore, so, calmly and quietly, do the fields of corn, the rounded tops **of** the fruit-laden trees, the ever-abiding flowers and flowering shrubs with which **the** country-side is decked, wave all over the land, whilst the sombre-suited native trees fill with beauty the whole country-side. Whether delving in the mine, fishing in the sea, ploughing the hill-sides, or attending to his herds of dairy cattle, the Australian of this part of **the** continent has always a pleasant scene to look upon and a profitable field of **labour to** engage in.

On rounding the lower head of Port Jackson **on the** journey down south, the village of Waverley is almost immediately **met** with. There are few

THE WATERFALLS.   139

platform, the engines are then reversed, and so, foot by foot, the highest ridges of the mountains are attained. Once on the summit of the hills, the railway passes along the mountain-tops, and at an elevation of 3,700 feet the Clarence tunnel is passed through. For over sixty miles of the mountain journey the traveller can see on either side of him other mountains and forests, with here and there a turbulent stream dashing over the ledges of the rock, or rushing across the stony beds of deep dark valleys. After the railway has run a course of about eighty miles, it passes through a coal-bearing district, of which the principal town is Hartley, situate right in the heart of the hills. This place is destined to become one of very considerable importance. Already large quantities of kerosene are manufactured there; and now that access to the west is every day becoming more practicable, its treasures of coal will be largely utilised in the settlements on the lightly-timbered plains inland. The Falls of the Weatherboard are not far from Hartley, and nearer still there is a waterfall known as Govett's Leap. The air up in these mountain regions is of remarkable purity, and the settled places are sought after for the salubrity of the climate and the beauty of the scenery. Natural beauties abound in every direction; and wherever cultivation—always limited in extent—has taken place, the country possesses charms that may be sought for in vain in more easily accessible districts.

The descent from the mountains into the country of the western plains was a work of even more difficulty than the ascent from the rivers on the eastern side. Tunnels, bridges, and viaducts succeed each other at short intervals, and every mile of country travelled discloses fresh beauties and new objects of interest. The western line is not yet completed to Bathurst, and before this can take place the River Macquarie will have to be spanned by a bridge of considerable dimensions. This kind of difficulty is, however, made short work of in New South Wales; and the extension of the rail, not only to Bathurst, but to the far west beyond, will soon be an accomplished fact. A glance at the map will show how vast a stretch of country such a line of communication will open up, and how beneficial it must be to the trade of the eastern seaboard. Some day the Victorian line from Echuca and the New South Wales line may cross each other, and then the trade of the interior will be briskly competed for. When that day comes, and before it indeed, rivers and creeks will have been crossed, reservoirs formed, and wells sunk; here and there agricultural settlements will have been formed, the rich natural pastures of the country will have increased in richness, and instead of wool only, with beef and mutton as a matter of course, the waggons will be

140   AUSTRALIA ILLUSTRATED.

laden with casks of wine and oil, with bags of corn and maize; strange fruits will have been grown, new industries opened up, and well-to-do people **met with** in thousands in every direction. When once the best plans of conserving and utilising the rainfall of Australia are acted upon, the capacity of the interior of the country to increase in riches will be practically boundless.

Bathurst is unexceptionably the most important of the inland towns of New South Wales, and, its distance from the coast being considered, of the whole of Australia. The site of the town **was fixed upon by** Governor Macquarie, soon after the mountains were first crossed. **Its actual** establishment as a town took place in May, 1815, and it has continued to grow in importance ever since. It is laid out in the orthodox Australian style, with long, straight, and wide streets, having others of a similar character intersecting them at right angles. The plain upon which it is built is gently undulating in character, and through the heart of the whole there runs a watercourse, across which several of the streets are bridged. The country round Bathurst, in every direction, consists of undulating downs or plains. Agricultural and pastoral pursuits are followed on a very extensive scale, and **with the** most satisfactory results. The first settlers had fully one hundred **and** twenty square miles of country to select from, nearly every acre of which was ready for the plough, and of an exceeding rich quality. There was none of the tiresome and expensive grubbing and clearing, that forms so serious a drawback to the farmer in timbered countries, round Bathurst. It was a vast territory of ready-made farming land, that only required ordinary labour and care to make it a source of unfailing wealth. For fully ten months out of the year the climate of the Bathurst district is simply delicious. No doubt its elevated position—the plains are over 2,000 feet above the sea-level—has much to do with this, and it is luckily a natural advantage of which nothing can deprive it.

Agriculture and the breeding of sheep and cattle are by no means the only sources of wealth to Bathurst. Auriferous country abounds, and a large number of prosperous settlements exist upon the various gold-fields in the district. Not many large fortunes have been made by the diggers hereabouts, but the gold workings always employ a great number of men, and have the effect of adding to the general prosperity of the place. A merely passing view of the town will serve to indicate this. Evidences of it are apparent in every direction. Half a dozen denominations of Christians possess one or more churches of handsome construction and large proportions, erected for the purposes of their religion. Schools abound, and a special school of arts is one of the foremost features of the place. The banks are all of them capital specimens of architecture, and a large amount of business is transacted in them ; the press is well represented, there being two newspapers in the town ; the theatre is opened occasionally ; the hotels are sufficiently numerous— some people express an opinion to the effect that a less number indeed would suffice for the requirements of the town, but Bathurst is not peculiar in this respect, for the same thing is said of some other towns at home and in the colonies—the shops and stores well built and well supplied, and the place altogether has a thoroughly well-to-do look about it. The farms round about partake of this quality. They are well tilled and kept, the fences are substantial, the houses strongly built and well furnished, **the** gardens trimly trained, and abounding in all the home-flowers the Australian loves so well, as well as with a myriad others of which "home-keeping folks" know nothing, save by report ; the roads are well formed, and for the most part in excellent condition ; and, taken all for all, Bathurst may be accepted for as perfect a specimen of an inland town as any new country need desire to possess. It has all the comfort that a rich virgin soil yields to ordinary industry, and it is without many of the evils that other and more densely populated places suffer from.

When it is remembered that twenty years ago Bathurst—in common with a score of townships of lesser importance—was a small collection of weatherboard houses, deriving its chief, importance from the fact **that it** formed a convenient resting-place for an occasional traveller ; that **access to** it from the eastern seaboard was only attainable by means of a **solitary road** carried along **the side of** precipitous ranges, over mountain **streams, and** across dangerous gorges, whilst the approach from the west was **over vast** monotonous-looking, and in some places sterile plains, the south being separated from it by a rugged range of mountains—its existence in its present state may be fairly looked upon as a development of social phenomena of which old-world people have only a very vague conception. Every year adds to its importance. The power of knowledge that teaches men to utilise natural gifts in the shape of rainfall and river beds is operating day by day. The legends of hot winds, unproductive plains, and weary wastes of scrub, are, one by one, giving way to the common experiences of every-day life and the honest determination of men bent upon making homes that shall be abiding-places in the widest and best sense of the word.

Everything is working, with that subtle wisdom that the watching of the works of nature teaches, towards this. All the convenient bends and turns and

matters of special importance attached to the place, although it is pleasantly situate, and the views obtainable from it of considerable beauty. Mansions, villas, tea-gardens, and hotels, rank among its chief characteristics, and its population numbers, perhaps, 1,000 or more. Randwick is a place of much greater importance. Here the Bishop of Sydney resides, and near here the chief racing meeting of the colony is held. Randwick race-ground is the model course of the colony, and travellers desiring to see the Sydney native in his glory should by no means omit visiting it during the racing season. He will come away with a high opinion of Australian racers and racing. The village—or rather town, for it is governed by a municipal council—of Randwick is placed very pleasantly as to position. It lies high and dry on the top of the heights called by the same name as the town. On one side a pretty valley, Waterloo by name, stretches away, bounded by the superior heights of Sydney itself. On the opposite side a view of the Vale of Waverley and the pleasant Bay of Coogee, into which the rollers of the Pacific break with more than usual force, is obtained, whilst the ocean forms a boundary of beauty beyond. Randwick is a favourite place of residence with Sydney merchants, and should perhaps have been spoken of in connection with the description of the city itself; but to include it within the coast districts seemed the more convenient plan. Hence the reference to it here.

Botany Bay is the next point of interest on the line of travel south; but sufficient has already been said to indicate its chief characteristics. The place is rich in memories, and richer still in natural beauty. Wherever a resting place for a patch of soil can be found on or around Botany Bay, there springs a plant, well-looking and handsome often, sometimes stunted and bare-looking enough, but always possessing that indescribable beauty that leaves of trees and petals of flowers bear upon them as a patent of nobility conferred by Nature herself. The visit of Cook to Botany Bay has already been referred to, as well as his meeting with the French navigator, La Perouse, in the same waters. About the last memorial of the French navigator is to be found on the shores of Botany Bay; for after he left there all traces of him were lost. A monument bearing the following inscription has been erected to his memory: "A la mémoire de Monsieur de la Perouse. Cette terre, qu'il visita en 1788, est la dernière d'où il a fait parvenir le ses nouvelles. Erigé au nom de la France par les soins de MM. Arugainville et Ducampier, commandant la frégate La Thétis, et la corvette L'Espérance, en relâche au Port Jackson en 1825. Le fondement posé en 1825; élevé 1828." Macquarie

Tower, of all others the **classic spot of Australia, is not far away from here.**

Port Hacking **is the** first considerable indentation on **the** coast south of Botany Bay. It makes a capital harbour for small craft, and would doubtless be utilised, and settlement take place round about, but for the dense scrub by which its waters are surrounded. This scrub makes capital cover for game, and good sport in hunting the wallaby may always be obtained in the neighbourhood. In thus affording field for relaxation, **it,** perhaps, serves as important a purpose **as** though its rich loamy bottoms **were** laid bare **and** maize and lucerne grown thereon.

From Wollongong—or rather from Bulli, a **small** inlet of **the** sea a few miles north of Wollongong—down to the Shoalhaven River, there extends a country of extreme beauty and fertility. It has fortunately been allowed to retain its native name, and the soft, liquid sound of Illawarra appears **to** convey some idea of the beauty of the place itself. It abounds in rich pasture-lands, watered by perpetual streams, is backed by a mountain range timbered with valuable woods, and bearing beneath the surface coal measures **more** valuable still. "Free selection" and settlement have sadly thinned the **timber;** and, indeed, before free selection, as understood nowadays, was ever **thought of, the most** valuable forest trees—the cedar of Australia, equal in **beauty and durability to the** mahogany of **other countries—was** nearly all exhausted. Thirty years ago the chief of the giant trees of the Illawarra forests were felled and turned into money. How valuable a wood is the cedar may be judged from the fact, that refuse logs are now and then found lying on the sides of Mount Keira, buried beneath a dense growth of creepers, mosses, and ferns, with the wood retaining all its original qualities of richness of colour and solidity of grain. They are, indeed, as sound as any "heart of oak," however carefully it may have been preserved and tended.

This, perhaps, will be as convenient a place as any to refer to the fact that no country in the world has been more highly favoured by nature in the abundance and variety of its timber-producing trees than New South Wales. On the west coast of the continent, indeed, larger forests and larger trees are found, yet the element of variety of kind to the same extent is wanting. From the district of Illawarra itself the forests have nearly disappeared, but a few years ago the whole of the district was covered with magnificent forests containing as great a variety of trees as any part of New South Wales. Many such districts remain, but settlement lessens their number day by day. The undergrowth of these forests is exceedingly beautiful in form and variety

TIMBER TREES. 147

of character. Some of the climbers twist and turn up and around the trunks of the larger trees, and so encompass and envelop them, that little of the original remains. A somewhat remarkable instance of this description of the freaks of nature may be seen near a small bridge some three or four miles away from the township of Wollongong. It is called the Giant Fig Tree, and a very handsome specimen of its kind it is. The original trunk appears to have been completely absorbed by climbing parasites, and these again, descending, have taken root and formed a mass of life quite distinct from the original tree itself. Among the other trees of the colony may be named the black apple, a tree beautiful in form, outline, and foliage. It bears a fruit something like a plum in shape, but having an insipid flavour. The wood is admirably adapted for cabinet work, having a fantastic grain running through it. The red ash is a handsome and useful tree, attaining a height of 100 feet, and giving wood used for a variety of purposes. The red cedar is, however, the king of trees in this part of the world. It is tall, averaging 150 feet, with a diameter of about 10 feet. Some of the best specimens of these trees have yielded upwards of 30,000 feet of merchantable timber. The coach-wood, so called because its timber is greatly in request for coachmaking purposes, is another beautiful tree, having a long straight stem. The wood is soft, easily worked, close in the grain, and emits an agreeable perfume. In this respect it resembles many other trees of the colony, notably the myall, a tree only found in the open parts of the country. It is shrub-like in its character, and its wood is in great request because of the violet scent by which it is distinguished, and because of which the timber is sometimes called violet-wood. Smokers who pride themselves on their pipes greatly affect the myall, and thousands of wooden pipes are sold in London perfumed and coloured so as to imitate it. The laurel or white sycamore, pretty plentifully distributed over the whole coast lands of New South Wales, has, when cut and worked in a green state, a powerfully aromatic fragrance, which however leaves it as the wood becomes old. The sassafras is a tree of exceeding beauty, bearing a foliage of dense glossy leaves, and emitting whilst growing an agreeable fragrance. Its bark is held in repute for certain tonic properties it is said to possess. The cork-wood is so called because of the character of its bark. Its chief value arises, however, from its wood being suitable for wood-engraving purposes. The timber of the rose-wood is also used by wood engravers, and it also emits an agreeable perfume. The mountain ash is tolerably plentiful in the Illawarra district, its wood is easily worked, and is chiefly used for making oars. The white beech is a truly noble tree. It has no great diameter—3 or 4 feet at the outside—but it frequently rises sheer up for 150 feet. Its wood is distinguished by a silvery white grain, and is much prized for flooring and the decks of ships. The white pine is held in great repute for flooring and for some cabinet purposes. It grows with a long straight trunk, sometimes attaining a height of 120 feet, and having a diameter of from 2 to 3 feet. The maiden's blush is one of the most beautiful of the forest beauties of Australia. It is a tree of moderate size, and is covered with large glossy leaves, which cluster together at the end of long pendulous branches. Its name is derived from the pale pinky hue of the wood. The silky oak is another very valuable tree. The wood is a beautiful red colour, with a close and fine grain. There are two different trees called apple-trees, though why or wherefore it is difficult to tell. They both belong to the myrtle family, both handsome, well-grown trees, yielding a timber very useful for many purposes. The blue gum is perhaps as pleasant a looking tree as any in the colony. Its leaves have a changeable purplish blush upon them, and make a shade very grateful during the warm Australian summer. Its timber is said to be better adapted for shipbuilding purposes than any other on the Australian continent. The ironbark is a grand-looking tree. A forest of ironbark trees has been thus described.*—" Black and grimy and hard were they, as the metal from which they take their name. The deep cracks and fissures in the rugged bark were filled with a black glittering gum, that seemed as though molten iron had been run into them. Their trunks rose up straight and tall and strong, whilst their branches and crowns were clothed with a mass of heavy dark foliage." To this may be added that this grand eucalyptus attains a height of 150 feet, with a diameter of from 4 to 5 feet. It is characterised by a straight even bole, and its timber is held in the highest possible repute for nearly every purpose where great strength is required. In consequence of its hardness the wood is difficult to work, but whenever it has been used for other than the roughest purposes, the result has more than repaid the labour bestowed upon it. The peppermint is another handsome tree; its timber is not so valuable as that of the ironbark, but is useful for a variety of purposes nevertheless. This tree is sometimes called the stringy bark, sometimes the red and again the white gum. The messmate is an immense tree, produces excellent timber, and is used for a great variety of ordinary purposes. The black-butt, or flintwood, runs up sometimes 200 feet. It has a dark-coloured rough bark at the base, becoming

* "Another England," 1st edition, p. 51.

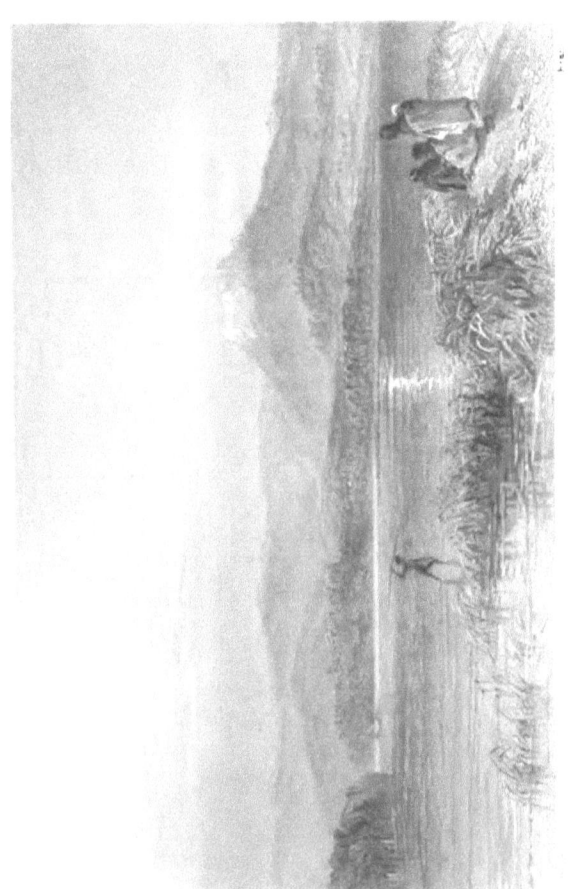

TOM IREDALE AMDH. HUSSEY SAMUEL HAYS.

gradually smoother, and falling off in long flakes towards the top. **There are half a dozen or** more of myrtles called tea-tree—prickly-leaved tea-tree, white tea-tree, and by several other names, these varying in various localities. Of the prickly-leaved tea-tree, it is said that the wood has never been known **to decay.** Whether this be the case or no, its durability has in numberless instances stood the test of **more** than half a hundred years. A good deal **further** south than the Illawarra district the white box is found, and of the **timber** of this **tree it** is said, that ribs of vessels formed of it have been found perfectly sound after a lapse of constant voyaging extending over **thirty years.** How much longer they may last it would be difficult **to tell.** ' **Of the trees** called wattle—they are all **acacias—it would be hard to count the number.** They are all small trees—shrubs would perhaps be the **most descriptive** name for them—but very beautiful in outline and colour. **Whether white or** red, silver or golden, the wattle is always beautiful. **Its blossoms** have a most delicate perfume, and its bark distils a valuable gum. It grows and flourishes in every direction, and is always a pleasant thing to look upon. A clump of wattles is as handsome an adjunct to a garden or park as can well be imagined, and the Australian, **as a** rule, is proud of and pleased with it.

When we come to speak of Queensland, Northern Australia, and the West Coast of the continent, there will be many trees, having special characteristics, to be spoken of; but in the meantime those referred to will serve to **convey a** tolerably tangible **idea** of the forest riches **of** Australia. How these **riches** are being utilised **may** be gathered from **the fact that** fully 500,000 feet **of** native timber **are either** used in or **exported from** New South Wales every week. At a moderate calculation **this timber realises** 20s. for **every** 100 superficial feet, having a thickness of one inch. Ironbark **is** sold in square **logs** at an average of about 3s. per cubic foot; wood for staves, and such like purposes, is sold at from £4 to £7 per thousand, and **shingles at** about 30s. for the same number. From these statements it will be seen that the native timber trade of the colony is an important and profitable one.

The views of Mount Keira, Tom Thumb's Lagoon—so called after the little **boat in which Bass** made his celebrated discovery—and the gully at Wollongong, convey, far better than any words can, some of the various phases of beauty with which this highly favoured district abounds. Mount Keira runs up sheer and precipitous for fully 1,500 feet. From its base the Vale **of** Illawarra stretches away to the south, and comprises a scene of loveliness not often equalled, even in Australia. From the summit of the hill the panorama is lovely in the extreme. Looking seaward, the "Five Islands" and the picturesque outline of the coast add a charm peculiarly their own, and of exceeding beauty. A road has been cut in the face of the cliff that forms one side of the hill, and the traveller, during the journey from Sydney to Wollongong, has many opportunities of viewing scenery of an exquisite and ever-changing beauty. The illustration, "The Gully **at Wollongong**," conveys a good idea of some of the out-of-the-way **places in the country.** The top of the mountain is even now well timbered, and the sides of the ranges covered with numerous varieties **of semi-tropical trees and plants.** Tom Thumb's Lagoon is a small inlet of the sea, **and is a thoroughly characteristic** bit of Australian scenery. The forests are not so dense **now as when the** sketch was taken, and the blackfellow, with his lubra and piccaninny, have become things of the past; but the high, precipitous mount, the gently rising hills, and far-spreading vales remain, and all the old beauty remains with **them still.**

Two or three miles north of Tom Thumb's Lagoon, and about forty miles south of Sydney, is the harbour and township of Wollongong. Until the **discovery** of coal—the coal-mines of the district are now of exceeding and of daily increasing **value—save the** beauty of the neighbourhood, there **was** nothing of special importance attached either to the township or the harbour. It has for many years been the shipping place for a rich agricultural district; and the port has always been considered a good one for refuge. **The** Belmore Basin is a work of considerable importance, and has been called into existence chiefly in consequence of the trade in coal. This basin has been excavated out of the solid rock, and measures 450 feet in length, by a breadth of 150. **It has been so arranged that** the **coal vessels can** take in **their** loading direct from the trucks as they leave the pit's mouth. **A breakwater** has been constructed across the **harbour, and just** off its mouth a lighthouse erected. The town is pleasantly situate at **the head** of the harbour, just above where the waters of the Macquarie Creek are discharged into it. There are churches, schools, hotels, stores, and places of business in plenty in Wollongong, and the place and neighbourhood possess all **the elements of** permanent prosperity.

Lake Illawarra is a considerable indentation in the coast, a little to the south of Tom Thumb's Lagoon, and after passing it and Point Bass the pleasantly situated seaport of Kiama is reached. The country round about is a real "land of Goshen," and is greatly celebrated, as is indeed every farm and village in the district, for the excellence of its dairy produce. From Shellharbour, **a** village in the district of Kiama, butter of good quality has

been imported into England. Like most other places possessing the advantage of building-stone easily attainable, Kiama has an important look about it, often wanting in places of greater importance. The churches have quite a handsome appearance, as have also several of the banks and places of business. A capital dock and breakwater have been erected, and the place always presents a tolerably lively appearance. Not far from the town, and between it and the beach, there is a somewhat singular formation that sometimes causes an interesting change in the ordinary quietude of the place. A rocky hill, of no very great height, is perforated from top to bottom—that is, from **the** surface to below high-water level—with a wide chimney-like **aperture. At** the top it is about fifteen feet in diameter, **but this increases towards the** bottom of the shaft. From this shaft there **runs a** passage **to the beach** beyond the cliffs that intervene. Whenever the wind **blows strongly from** the east—and considering the thousands of miles of water it sweeps across, it is not difficult to imagine it blowing pretty stiffly now and then—the waters are forced up this passage, and, on arriving at the foot of the "blow-hole," they seethe, and boil, and roar, and then, forcing themselves up with a mighty noise, as though a school of whales had got imprisoned in the caverns below, rise in a grand column that the winds drive in Scotch-like mists over **the** neighbouring lands. A few miles west of Kiama, or, rather, west of Wollongong, an iron and coal-bearing country extends, and in the midst of it are the celebrated Fitzroy Iron Works, at Nattai. Large sums of **money have been** spent upon these works, but hitherto the result has been little short of disastrous. Opinions differ as to the reason of this, for coal and iron, both of good quality, lie close together, and the district is connected with the metropolis by rail. **On the** line of rail near Nattai occurs the longest railway tunnel in the colony, running through a hill called Gibraltar, not unlike the famous rock from which it takes its name.

The Shoalhaven River empties itself into the Pacific a few miles to the south of Kiama. This is by far the most important stream on the coast south of Sydney. It takes its rise in the Coromboro Swamp, at an elevation of nearly 3,000 feet above the sea. Its head-waters run through a country of singularly romantic beauty. In some places it winds through valleys—the Shoalhaven glens they are called—the sides of which vary in height from 500 to 1,500 feet. Gold-diggings abound in the upper part of the river, and many settlements of agriculturists. As the stream nears the sea its banks become flat, and are liable to inundation, sometimes of a very serious character. Not far from its mouth, Mount Coulangatta, 1,000 feet high, rises and forms a capital landmark for voyagers. Although the Shoalhaven is navigable for some distance, the entrance to the river is effected by way of Crookhaven River, an arm of the Shoalhaven, having the advantage of being protected from the south-easterly gales by a rocky headland, down to the north head of Jervis Bay. This is the largest sheet of sheltered water on the New South Wales coast, and is capable of affording refuge to 200 sail of ships. On one side of the two-mile wide entrance to Jervis Bay, there **is a** somewhat **singular** formation called Mount Perpendicular. This point rises abruptly from the sea for 200 feet, and runs away to the north, having a steep wall-like face the whole way to Point Beecroft. South of the entrance to Jervis Bay is Cape George, and a little further south still an irregularly-shaped bay called Sussex Haven. Eighteen or twenty miles south of Cape George one of the safest harbours in the colony is met with. Ulladulla it is called, and a thoroughly pleasant place it is. How pleasant can best be told by those who **may, by stress of weather, have** had to throw themselves upon the hospitality **of the inhabitants.** This hospitality has never **been** known to fail. Ulladulla is a prosperous as well as a pleasant place. At one time ship-building was carried on to a limited extent, but of late years the industry has been discontinued. The surrounding country is undulating, and good soil is more frequently met with than bad. In common with all the other places on this part of the coast, it is noted for the quality of its butter. Burril Lake, an expanse of salt water about seven miles long, affords capital sport to the bearers of either gun or rod. Its waters abound with schnapper and whiting, and its banks with wild fowl in plenty. It was from Ulladulla that the porcelain clay, to which was awarded the gold medal at the London Exhibition of 1862, was forwarded. Some day this clay will doubtless be worked with profit. At present the population is too small, and other pursuits too profitable, to allow much attention to be paid to pottery.

In connection with the next points of interest on the coast, Bateman's Bay and the Moruya and Tuross Rivers, it will be as well for the sake of compactness to say a word or two on the towns of the gold-fields that lie in this direction. Apart from its gold-bearing character, there is little to interest the reader, although the country is in many parts very beautiful. The sketch **of** Broulee is thoroughly characteristic of some portions of the district. The nearest town of any importance to Bateman's Bay is Araluen, the centre of a prosperous gold-digging district. Braidwood is a more important town still, and is situate on the banks of the Shoalhaven River. The country around Braidwood is of a good agricultural character, and is tolerably well settled upon.

Most of the land is in private hands, so that free selection is a thing not much **known**. The wheat grown **in** the neighbourhood is held in high esteem, and **is, as a** rule, a profitable crop. Sometimes the rust gets into it, and then loss ensues. Queanbeyan **is** further west than Braidwood, and gains its importance from being the chief town of a district called by the same name. Round about all these places gold is obtained. The country is, however, not easily accessible, and road-making across or around the mountains a question of considerable expense. The Tuross River flows through what are called the Gulf gold-fields. The mouth of this river would form a capital outlet for the produce, mineral and otherwise, of a very important district, were it not for a shifting-bar that prevents navigation. This drawback will doubtless be removed by-and-by. Nerrigundah, the chief town of the Gulf gold-fields, is most pleasantly situated in a long narrow valley shut in on every side by steep ranges, and possesses a peculiarly mild and salubrious climate.

After the Tuross comes the Dry River. Why so called it would be difficult to say, for it is a tolerably large stream, although it flows through a scrubby and rugged country. The Bega succeeds to the Dry River, and this also is an important and a useful stream. The town of Bega is situate at the junction of the Bemboka and the Bega rivers, these streams after this point taking the name of the Bega. The country round about Bega is thoroughly home-like in character. It consists of low-lying and gently-undulating hills, not unlike those that run in some places between the counties of Sussex and Kent. Farms abound hereabout, and comfortable homesteads are to be met with in every direction.

Twofold Bay, Cape Howe excepted, is the last place of importance on the coast of New South Wales south of Sydney. There is nothing particularly striking in the appearance of Twofold Bay. The shores are of moderate elevation, broken into steep points and stretches of sandy beach. There are capital fishing-grounds both in and outside the bay, and in the proper season a good number of the inhabitants devote themselves to whaling. The only settlement of any importance on the shores of the bay is the small township of Eden. This little place is the port for the whole of the south-eastern district of New South Wales, and the trade is almost as unimportant as the place itself. The surrounding country is rugged, and only in isolated patches adapted for agriculture. There is a meat-preserving establishment not far from Eden, and the place is as self-contained a spot as could well be imagined. From Twofold Bay to Cape Howe is not far, nor is there any point on the **coast** between calling for special notice. Taking Cape Howe as the apex of an irregularly-shaped triangle, having Wagga Wagga—made notorious, if not celebrated, in the records of the Tichborne trial—for its western, and the city of Goulburn for its eastern extremity, there lies a district, having several places of importance within its borders, to which only partial reference has been made. A rhomboidal block of land running through the heart of the triangle referred to comprises the pastoral district of Maneroo, or Monaro, as the authorities have of late taken to spelling it. The Monaro Plains, or Downs, for the latter term describes them best, are composed of richly-grassed, undulating stretches of country, bounded on either side by hills, sometimes wild and almost inaccessible, but in other places rising gently, and having lightly-timbered and easily-cultivated sides. The central, that is the level, portion of this district forms a plateau more than seventy miles long, is tolerably well settled, and good crops, chiefly cereals, are raised upon it.

Travelling northward across the Delegate Mountains from Cape Howe, the first township met with is Bombola, around which pastoral and agricultural pursuits are successfully carried on. Gold, lead, and copper mines have all been worked within short distances of the town, and have added materially to its prosperity. On the track from Bombola to Cooma, the Snowy Mountains, with Kosciusko towering above them all, may be seen on the west, the intervening country being composed of the undulating plains and moderately high hills already spoken of. Cooma is quite an important and a flourishing place. There are patches of rich agricultural land in every direction round about, and the mixture of basalt and granite, with the attendant flora, combine to form a district of unusual and romantic beauty. There is a capital hospital and benevolent asylum in the town, besides a literary institute, all the ordinary public offices, a capital newspaper, and the usual number of hotels. Settlement has taken place to a very considerable extent, the practice of "free selection" having been largely pursued by the gold-miners and others living in and around the township. There are several rivers within a convenient distance of Cooma, which may be taken as the centre of the rhomboid of Monaro. The Kiandra gold-fields lie to the north-west of Cooma, situate in the heart of a heavy mountainous country. Kiandra was the scene of a large "rush" of gold-diggers from Victoria and elsewhere a good many years ago. The story of the toil, the suffering, and the loss of those who passed over the snowy regions and rocky defiles in order to reach Kiandra has been often told, and is only one in a long catalogue of "vain hopes and tired endeavour." Kiandra is scarcely ever heard of now; but it

will be some day again, for the hills and water-courses round about are rich in the richest of all mineral treasures.

Passing over the western boundary of Monaro, and into the district of the Murrumbidgee, Tumut, a rich agricultural, and Adelong, an old gold-mining district, is met with. A few miles westward of the latter place, is Wagga Wagga, situate on the main road from Albury to Sydney. Turning to the east, and running up the river, Gundagai is reached; and this is by far the most interesting settlement to be met with on the banks of the Murrumbidgee. It is the **furthest point in the interior of** Australia to which navigation from the sea **has hitherto been found practicable.** Steamers have been in the habit of **trading to it from Adelaide ever** since the spring of 1868. In the September of **that year, Captain Francis** Cadell, to whose untiring exertion the opening up **of the navigable streams** of the southern parts of Australia is almost, if not altogether, due, warped a steamer alongside the banks of the Murrumbidgee at Gundagai. The importance of this may be easily estimated from the fact that, by way of the Murrumbidgee and the Murray, the journey to the sea-board at Adelaide is accomplished in about a fortnight, and that the journey overland, either to Sydney or Melbourne, often took as many weeks as the steamer required days for its passage. The facilities afforded by the river voyage for the transmission of wool from the districts north of the Murrumbidgee and the Lachlan must have had a very considerable effect towards developing the pastoral industries of Riverina and the districts beyond.

Gundagai has, however, an interest pertaining to it **arising from other** and more perfectly natural causes. Although a township **at the point of the** river now known as Gundagai was first suggested in 1836, and the survey of the town made in 1840, it was not until three years afterwards that settlement of any importance took place on the spot. In 1844, the desirability of founding a township on that part of the river was somewhat seriously questioned, in consequence of a flood coming down the river and submerging the whole district to an average depth of four feet. On that occasion no lives were lost, and the flood being chiefly caused by the back-water, comparatively little damage was done. Year after year the same calamity occurred, but the effect upon the inhabitants was of the slightest possible character. The people seemed to take a delight in tempting and then dodging the flood. In the interval they would plough their lands and sow their seeds, reap their crops and stack their wheat and oats and barley. When the "latter rains" began to fall, they felt some doubt, but when inch by inch and foot by foot the river rose, their doubts all departed, and they began to pick out each his favourite **tree**, in the branches of which they proposed taking refuge. Some **were content to trust to the frail safety of** the ridge-poles of their **houses, and** many a miserable night, not unaccompanied by danger, have **the people of** Gundagai passed, sitting on the branches of trees or clinging to the more treacherous strength of a badly-built chimney. Thus **things went on until** the mid-winter—that is the June—of 1852. In that **month, the rain** descended, and the floods rushed down, with more than usual force. **Nothing,** save a vast waste of water, was to be seen for miles and **miles round about** Gundagai. The town then consisted of about eighty **houses**; when the water subsided, half a dozen of them remained, and they were severely damaged. Fully a hundred people were drowned, whilst sheep and cattle were swept away in hundreds and thousands. This last calamity had the **effect of making** people move a little further away from the river, and the **present township is** in a sufficiently safe and comfortable position. Some of **the** old inhabitants who remain grudge the few hundred yards extra over which they have to draw their water; but, as a rule, the people of Gundagai are fully alive to the advantages of a town allotment situate above the highest water-mark.

After the great south road has been followed for about forty miles, Yass, a capital specimen of an Australian up-country town, is reached. It has its main street, clean and capacious as a street need be, besides several others running into it at right angles. There are numerous public buildings of considerable importance, plenty of hotels, a newspaper, a hospital, and mechanics' institute and reading-room; it is in direct telegraphic and post communication with the neighbouring colonies, and is surrounded by a rich and improving district. On three sides the plain, on the westerly edge of which the town is situate, is sheltered and overlooked by mountains, Mount Bowing, a conical well-wooded hill, being the most prominent point of the range. Metals have been found in various directions round about the town, and at the junction of the Yass and Murrumbidgee rivers, silver has been discovered in considerable quantities. Pastoral and agricultural pursuits, in connection with the trade naturally pertaining to a town situate on the main line of traffic between two important colonies, compose the chief elements of well-doing to Yass and its neighbourhood.

South of Yass, and of a much more important town to which reference will have to be made presently, is Lake George, the largest sheet of water on the table land of the colony. The lake **is** situate on the very crown of the plateau, more than 2,000 feet above the level of the sea, and surrounded by mountains, some of them rising nearly as high above its waters as they are above the ocean. Lake George is twenty miles long, with an average width of seven miles. It is a perfect sea in miniature, has its bays and headlands, sandy benches, rocky projections, and sheltered vales, upon whose pebbly strands the waters roll when the wind ruffles, and by which they flow quietly when the elements are still. Many pleasant homes are to be found in its neighbourhood, chiefly towards the village of Bungendore, not far from the lower, and Collector, a settlement about two miles above the highest point of the lake. On either side, that is to say, on the east and west, the mountains run up from the edge of the water, and increasing in height as they recede inland on the one side, and towards the coast on the other, at length tower up as though intended to prevent intrusion from the outer world.

Wild fowl of every description are plentiful on Lake George, and its waters literally teem with fish—"strange fish" some of them, for the platypus is often met with, and the "debbil debbil" of the natives, a kind of seal, sometimes approaches the surface and affrights the passer-by. The waters of the lake, if not salt, are at any rate brackish. This is caused by the surface-water percolating through soils holding salts in solution. These accumulate year by year, and some would-be wise people have propounded strange theories thereupon, including one to the effect that the Pacific manages to make for itself an underground passage into the lake. All the scenery around is of an exceedingly interesting character, and the far-off "cloud-capped towers," covered with perpetual snow, give an additional interest to the scene. Lake Bathurst, a sheet of water similar in character, but scarcely half the size of Lake George, is situate on the east side of the Dividing Range, and about a dozen miles away.

Goulburn, an episcopal city, lies twenty-five miles south of the lake, between which and the city a series of rich plains extend. Goulburn possesses all the adjuncts and appliances of an important city. It is surrounded by a mining and agricultural district of great value, its public buildings are handsome specimens of architecture, its newspapers held in good repute, its people prosperous, and its importance increasing. From Goulburn the Southern Railway runs to Sydney. Southward it is intended to extend it to Albury, on the Victorian border. The country between Goulburn and the capital has been already sufficiently referred to, and we leave New South Wales as we entered it—by way of the "Queen City of the South."

CHAPTER XVII.

QUEENSLAND.

SYSTEMATIC EMIGRATION.—ITS FAILURE.—A GUARANTEE OF SUCCESS.—EARLY
CONDITION OF QUEENSLAND.—THE SURVEY OF FLINDERS.—THE NATIVES
THEIR TREATMENT.—CONVICTS' SEPARATION.—LOCAL SELF-GOVERNMENT.
THE MACROSSES.—A LONG JOURNEY.—THE LAND OF PROMISE.—THE RELIEF.

A good deal has been talked and **written** about "systematic **emigration.**"
By this phrase is meant, as a rule, the deportation of **men and women from**
one part of the earth's surface, where they **find it hard to live, to another,**
where the conditions of life are comparatively **easy and pleasant.** Well-
meaning and benevolent people, sad and sorry **at the suffering** they **see**
around them, too often, take it for granted that any change must be for the
better, and seem to think that the fact of a man being **poor, of** having
inherited or achieved misfortune, is qualification sufficient to enable him to
arrive at, by some royal but ill-defined road, the condition of a prosperous
and valuable colonist. Practical experience teaches that, as a rule, and under
such circumstances, the very causes that have made or kept him poor at home
will be constant sources of failure to him in a new country. Notwithstanding
this, every winter, and, indeed, all the year round, emigration societies **are**
planned, promoted, and established. Money is spent, systems organized, the
Government prayed and petitioned, sometimes threatened, because, say the
well-meaning but utterly mistaken promoters, emigration, to be effective for
good, must be systematic, and men and women must be sent abroad in
masses. For the most part all such systems have failed, and, for those most
directly concerned, failed most miserably and cruelly. This applies to
nearly every scheme of so-called systematic emigration, and in no instance
more entirely, cruelly, and miserably than when women and children have
been the objects of deportative benevolence. Every British colony has
afforded examples of the evils resulting from sending people abroad for the
simple reason that they were not doing well at home. Every successful
attempt at colonisation has been brought about by individual energy, and
so-called systems have, as a rule, been the chief drawbacks to their prosperity. The first step towards success as a colonist consists in a man
attempting to help himself out of the surroundings of his ordinary existence,
and he who does this gives a guarantee of his probable success in the new
home he endeavours to make.

FIRST DISCOVERIES.

The history of **the colony of Queensland** offers a practical and striking **example** of the **truth of this doctrine.** Up till 1859 this vast territory **formed portion of the** colony of New South Wales. Until the previous year, **the district had** been little known, and, perhaps, less cared for. It was then an almost purely pastoral country. There were three or four towns within its borders. Brisbane was, as it continues to be, the chief of these. The stations of the squatters lay far apart from each other. **In** those times **a** man might ride from morn to night on a long December day, and keeping **a** river as his guide—the Fitzroy, for instance—remain within the boundaries **of** his own **run the** whole time; the back country, to which he could lay claim, often extending into parts unknown, and its extent defined on a map merely. Moreton Bay—so the northern districts of New South Wales were called—extended from 10 degrees south to the 29th degree of the same latitude. From the Pacific on the coast, it ran westward to the 138th degree of east longitude, and included a country nearly a dozen times the size of that of England. During the first years of Australian colonisation, little was done in the north-eastern portion of the country. About twelve years after the settlement of New South Wales, an examination of the north-eastern coasts was made. The information arising therefrom was not very definite. Now and then a traveller would return—as was the case with the boatmen who reported the discovery of coal on the beach far away to the north of the Hunter—and tell strange stories; but, save in the records left by Cook, little was known about the country. In the last year of the last century it was determined to send out an expedition for the purpose of obtaining information, chiefly with reference to the character of the bays and ports of the coast. Charge of the expedition was entrusted to Lieutenant Flinders, who, in the previous year, had been connected with Bass in the labour that resulted in defining Tasmania as an island, and the discovery of the straits between that colony and Victoria. The record of Flinders's voyage to the north is a most interesting one. He met with many natives, found them far advanced in the arts of peace, when compared with their brethren in the Port Jackson district; **he** talked and traded with them, and returned home deeply impressed with the many excellences of character displayed by them. Their houses **or huts were well** built, and excellently adapted for the purposes they were intended to serve. Both men and women were industrious and intelligent, were kindly in their disposition and manners, and were kindly treated in return by their first white visitors. The after-records of the same country contain chapters telling a different tale to this. Wholesale massacres, poisonings, and shootings must all be included in the list of incidents of subsequent exploration and settlement. Money making merely was not the sole object of the first explorers, and to this, perhaps, may be attributed their happier relations with the natives.

Notwithstanding that the result of Flinders's voyage showed that the coast-river was easily navigable, and that he described the northern portions of the colony as being eminently adapted for settlement, nearly a quarter of a century elapsed before his discoveries were utilised. By this time New South Wales was in a prosperous condition. The convict element was strong, but the inhabitants generally, including the old convicts themselves, were desirous that their number should not be added to. As a preliminary step towards the formation of a new settlement, a detachment of the 40th Regiment was sent to Moreton Bay. This was in 1824, and nearly simultaneous with the discovery of Port Phillip in the south. For eighteen or twenty years after the despatch of the 40th, the Moreton Bay district was used and looked upon as a purely penal settlement. During the whole of that period the experiences of the colonists were of a very terrible character. The mother country poured swarms of convicts into the district, and as a rule, the free men and women who found their way into it were little, if at all, better than their fellows held in bondage. The convict population was, however, not without certain advantages. During the continuance of the system in Moreton Bay, roads were made, bridges built, and buildings erected of a most substantial character. Lacking the bonded labour, many of them would probably never have had an existence, or, at any rate, not until very many years had passed. In 1842 the settlement became free, and now it is as little affected with the convict taint as England itself. As has been the case everywhere else, certain employers of labour desired a continuance of the system; but public opinion was too strong for them, and all the subsequent experience of the colony—and, indeed, of all other colonies—has tended to prove how undesirable an element imported convictism is, and how much better a country is without it.

Very early in the history of Moreton Bay the people settled there became impressed with the desirability of separating themselves, in all matters relating to government, from the southern colony—New South Wales. The agitation with reference to this separation commenced in 1847, or possibly earlier. It was carried on from year to year, and with more or less of vigour as circumstances seemed to point to its desirability, until the object sought was obtained. All Australians hold in high esteem a principle rapidly gaining ground among the people of the United Kingdom and of Europe generally, and that the Home Rulers of Ireland take as the motto of their measures, namely, that of local self-government. All over the settled portions of Australia, Shire, Borough, and Municipal councils are met with; in some instances, indeed, they are too closely packed together to render their working profitable. So soon as population spreads very far from the seat of government, one of the first things the pioneers busy themselves about is "setting up for themselves." Centralization finds little sympathy from the Australians whose abiding-places are removed beyond the influences of the improvements, in the shape of road and bridge making, effected by government funds, to which they contribute. This feeling is not unlikely to have a serious and unfavourable influence upon the attempt to establish a confederation of the colonies for a good many years to come. Already steps are being taken by the settlers in the northern parts of Queensland, with a view to separating themselves from those of the south, and constituting themselves into a Capricornus or Carpentaria, as the case may be. Even when this division takes place, the end will not have been arrived at, for assuredly the people of the north-east will desire to separate themselves from those of the north-west, and vice versa, whilst the latter will hardly care to have the seat of their government situate at Adelaide. When the extent of territory referred to is considered, these divisions of places will hardly be deemed unnatural, nor their accomplishment beyond the bounds of probability.

Although the early history of Queensland was not without its changes and excitements, it was not until the latter months of 1858 that the turning-point in its career was reached. The first steps on the road to permanent prosperity were entered upon in consequence of as ill-advised and unsystematic a rush of emigrants as any recorded in the whole history of colonisation. In its nature and results it overturns all the theories of the *doctrinaire* with reference to systems and plans as affecting colonisation, and is strongly suggestive of the adaptability of men to settle down wisely and well, under strange circumstances, if they only see sufficient inducement, are allowed sufficient scope, and not meddled and interfered with too much. The history of the early days of the progress of Queensland might easily be made to fill volumes of interesting and instructive matter. It will, however, best serve the present purpose to tell it briefly as may be.

The year 1858 was one of very considerable depression in the gold-fields of the older colonies. The large fortunes realised in the earlier days had, many of them, been spent, recklessly speculated with, or dissipated.

162   AUSTRALIA ILLUSTRATED.

The diggers had not yet learned to look upon their earnings or savings
with content. The implements of working were still primitive, and though gold,
alluvial and in quartz, existed in quantity, the appliances for obtaining it were
rude and methodless. As early as the summer of July of 1848 water for gold-
washing purposes began to be known as a long and dry summer was predicted.
If repeated and painful experiences of failure could have taught gold-diggers
wisdom, those of the northern parts of Australia would have been very wise
long before 1858. With the exception of the rush to the Woolshed Creek,
in the Ovens district, nearly every expedition to far-off fields in search of
gold had proved a failure. They were, as a rule, unfortunate, and in some
instances disastrous in their results. What was not to be known however,
or the time for its practice had not arrived. Omeo and Kiandra, the Snowy
River, and the Lachlan, had imparted their lessons in vain. A voyage across
the seas to Panama, ending in worse than disaster, and a deliberate fraud,
attended with much of loss of life and ruin, were all powerless to divert the
mind of the gold-digger from the desire to prove rich on a hurry. Just when
the miners were most likely to be easily affected, before their savings were
exhausted, and when the desire to make up for bygone losses was keen
upon them, news came to the effect that somewhere up in the north, far
beyond where diggers had ever been before, in a corner of the country
hitherto given up to sheep and cattle alone, gold, in plenty, and lying close
to the surface, had been discovered. The news spread as only such news
among such a people can. At first the information was of the most inde-
finite character imaginable. Nevertheless it told of an ever-flowing river,
of rich alluvial flats, and "made hills" having gold-bearing drifts and rocks
for their bases. This was said, too; of the actual whereabouts of the new
Dorado so little was at first known that the earlier sailing vessels were char-
tered for Port Curtis—a harbour considerably to the south of Keppel Bay.
This was soon remedied, however. Charts were looked up, and by the aid of
the experiences of masters employed in the international trade, and the directions given by the surveyors of 1861, Keppel Bay was decided upon as the
best port for the new gold-country, and into Keppel Bay, for some few weeks
successively, ships passed to search.

The fact that just at this time the ports of Sydney and Melbourne were
crammed with unemployed vessels, and among them some of the best ships
in the world, might have raised the suspicions of any class of men less credu-
lous than the gold-diggers of that day. But these things, and innumerable
cautions from the press, were powerless to restrain the exodus. It was

pointed out that from Batavia, and from the ports of India and China, came information of an almost utter lack of employment for ships existing, and that profitable freights for them could not be obtained. Little doubt could exist in the minds of any that the "rush" to Panama had been promoted entirely in the interest of shipowners and ship-agents, and this fact was insisted on over and over again—utterly without effect. Fast as ships were laid on the berth for Keppel Bay they were filled with gold-diggers and their appropriate surroundings. From every gold-field and up-country township, diggers flocked into Melbourne and Sydney in thousands. Quiet, easy-going South Australians and Tasmanians joined in the mad stampede, and within a month fully forty thousand men had been landed on the hitherto unthought-of shores of the river Fitzroy. In New South Wales and Victoria stage-coaches reaped a rich harvest. Colossal vehicles, each of them carrying from fifty to sixty passengers, started from all the more important towns to the coast, three or four a day. All the highways and many of the cross roads of the colonies, leading from the gold-fields towards the sea, were filled with lines of stalwart men, many of them carrying heavy weights upon their shoulders, bound in the same direction. Ships' agents had to improvise passenger-offices, in which clerks were employed taking passage money from morning till night. Day by day the crowds poured into the towns, and ships sailed from the ports, without any definite information having been received from the so much thought of new gold-diggings. When the diggers were asked their reasons for the migration, the most vague answers possible were given: somebody had heard of the discovery of gold, and given the information to some one else. This was sufficient: all the early glories of Ballarat, of Bendigo, and Forest Creek were to be repeated within the line of the tropics. Diggers gave up paying claims, clerks and shopmen relinquished situations, schemers and speculators were not wanting, nor, indeed, were worse characters than these latter utterly unknown; and had gold in quantity existed at Canoona, Rockhampton would have exhibited an example of one of the most speedily developed cities in the world.

The emigration from the southern colonies had continued for some six weeks, when positive intelligence of the failure of the Canoona gold-fields reached their centres of population. In Hobson's Bay the last ship had been filled with passengers, and started on her journey. As she was passing through the heads of Port Phillip, a returning steamer was entering. She was known to be from Keppel Bay, and the vessels were brought sufficiently close for the people on board both to speak to each other. To the question, asked with keen interest and breathless expectancy, "What news?" a loud and sustained warning to "go back" was returned. "No gold! a swindle!" was shouted again and again from hundreds of voices of men on board the homeward-bound steamer. The excitement on board the ship was intense. Men turned towards each other with undecided looks, which seemed to ask for advice as to the course to be **pursued, without** putting the question in articulate form. Meantime the ship and the steamer were drawing apart from each other, and as the last sounds of "Come back! come back!" from the latter to the former died away, the captain of the outward-bound one did the most sensible thing he could do under the circumstances. He offered to return at once to Melbourne and land his passengers, if they would resign all claim to the moneys they had paid. **The** offer was refused, and away the ship sped through the waters of Bass's **Straits with as "brave** a west wind" behind her as **ever blew wanderers home.** By the time Cape Howe was reached, the wind had veered round to **the south, and soon there** was a hurricane sufficiently strong to make it wise **to heave the** ship to for over twenty hours. This experience was not without the effect of inducing some of the passengers to desire to return to port. The ship was, however, under orders to proceed to China, and to return to Melbourne then would have involved a greater expenditure of money than to continue the passage north. Besides this the majority of the passengers were bent on "seeing the affair out," and the heel of the hurricane carried the ship into Keppel Bay on the evening of the eighth day after leaving Melbourne.

The scene that greeted the new-comers was an impressive one. For the previous four or five hours they had been sailing within sight of the shore. Between them and the mainland a long sandy island had extended. At the back of this the monotonously outlined and level mimosa-covered shores loomed sad-looking and strange. The land seemed to offer no very warm welcome to the adventurers. Just as the short twilight of Capricorn was changing to the clear darkness of the night, a break in the sand-hills that had for so long characterised the scene took place. Cape Capricorn, a tolerably bluff eminence when compared with the low surroundings, was in sight; **and soon** as the vessel's head was turned towards the west, three mount-like rocks were seen rising sheer and straight out of the water, looking as much like towers placed for purposes of defence as any fortification built by man could do. Soon as the shelter of the shore was reached, the long swell of the Pacific was left behind, and a clear lake-like sheet of water entered. By

this time the half-light had entirely faded away, and given place to the clear brilliancy of the stars: the anchor was dropped, and, **so far as** the ship was concerned, the adventurers were at their journey's end. **Of** course all eyes had been turned westward from the first; and as the last rays of the sun **faded** away over the land, they lit up the top timbers of a forest of masts **that marked the** position of a fleet of ships that lay farther in towards the **mouth of the river.**

That night was a strangely anxious one to the new-comers. From the **low-lying and weird-looking shore there came** mysterious sounds—the hum of winged insects, whilst **strange whispers seemed to float over the waters** of the bay, from the shadowy mimosæ with which the land was lined in **every** direction. The wash of the tide into the scarce-discernible creeks that ran into the bay from nearly every direction, and into the shallow passages between the long sandy island and the mainland, had, under the circumstances, a depressing and almost fearsome influence. The stars, great masses of steady yet brilliant light, were reflected deep down in the water, and lit up the sides of the tower-like rocks with a colouring rare and almost magical in **its richness.** From the forest and open lands beyond the mimosa-covered banks sounds of night-birds were wafted; now and then the distant bleating of sheep and lowing of cattle were heard; whilst above all the clear-sounding ship-bells told of the passing time. Nor was this sound the only messenger sent by the neighbouring ships. Occasionally a boat-load of men, who had travelled to the new diggings, tried them, and failed, came alongside; then the whole tale of failure, deeply coloured in all cases, was told, and the newly arrived ones sought their beds in great perplexity that night.

In connection with the circumstances and the time, as well as with the ship whose passage from Melbourne to the mouth of the Fitzroy has been narrated, there occurred a matter **that will serve** to illustrate, on a small scale, the fluctuating fortunes of money-seekers in those days. The bargain between the ship's agents and the passengers included the conveyance of the latter, by steamer, from Keppel Bay to Rockhampton. In order to carry out this part of the bargain, the agents had arranged with a Melbourne ship-owner to convey the passengers the distance referred to, at a cost of £1 each. Before the sailing of the steamer, however—on the evening of the sailing of the ship, indeed—the news of the failure of the new gold-fields had, as has been shown, been received, and the steamer was consequently not dispatched. At first it seemed impossible for the captain to carry out this part of the con-**tract; and he** offered to send his passengers up the river by sailing-schooners, of which there were several available. This offer was declined, the passengers being by no means anxious to arrive at a place from which they now knew they would have to take immediate steps for their return passage. The maintenance of one hundred men for an additional day or two makes a serious difference in the expenses of a ship, and it was desirable to land the passengers as early as possible. During the night rumours of a steamer being somewhere up the river, waiting, indeed, for the return-rush that was sure to take place, was received. The captain of the ship whose fortunes we have followed acted upon the information at once. He took a boat's crew, and was pulled up the stream. After rowing a few miles, he met with the steamer bringing the first downward cargo of passengers. A bargain for an upward freight of 6s. per head was soon struck, and by this the shipowner made an extra profit of £300, and the passengers, greatly to their own disgust and the delight of the captain, were landed at Rockhampton the same day.

The first dawn of the next morning saw the ship that had carried the first of those who joined in the "mad stampede" to the Canoona gold fields moved up to the ordinary anchorage of Keppel Bay, and within an hour she formed one of as fine a fleet of ships as the mercantile navy of the world could boast of. They hailed from every nautical nation in the world, and it was a singular sight to see the flags of the various nationalities streaming out to the wind in one of the most out-of-the-way corners of England's dominions. One little vessel was easily distinguishable from the rest, and gave a peculiar characteristic to the whole scene. A gun boat of the English royal navy was there, and her mere presence was all that was needed to keep in order one of the most heterogeneous crowds ever gathered together. The crowd was soon dispersed, and within a month the Fitzroy and the country round about—save for the remains of the camping-places on its banks, and the numberless holes that had been sunk in search of gold—had resumed its ordinary appearance. The story of the leaving of the country is almost as strange as that of the entrance thereto, but it need not be told here. Suffice it to say, that with the immigration of an undisciplined, disorganized, and unreasoning mass of men commenced the development of a colony so prosperous that its ultimate destiny overpowers the desire to prophecy its future greatness.

CHAPTER XVIII.

QUEENSLAND.—*Continued.*

LOOKING A-HEAD.—A PLEASANT LIFE.—AMATEUR SQUATTING.—UNFULFILLED HOPES.—THE MAD SEASON.—GOOD TIMES.—WANT OF LABOUR.—AN EMIGRATION LECTURER.—A PLEASANT FUTURE.—THE RIGHT AND WRONG EMIGRANTS.—FAILURE AND SUCCESS.—REVIVAL AND WORK.—THE FUTURE OF QUEENSLAND.

AMONG the thousands who sought the new gold-fields of the North there were some who looked beyond the failure that had attended their first efforts. It has been already said that affairs in the Southern colonies were none of the brightest. Speculation and overtrading had been accompanied or followed by disaster, and many of those who had joined in the rush to Queensland felt that their energies must find vent and employment otherwhere than in the colonies they had left. The natural riches of the new land were—the lack of gold notwithstanding—too palpable to be overlooked. The old settlers were few and far between, but they had prospered; and so a good many of the new-comers made up their minds to enter into that prosperity. Many of them were entirely destitute of means, and few, indeed, possessed of sufficient money to enable them to settle in a country of which the only cultivated products were horses, cattle, and sheep. They had "colonial experience," however, and this commodity, when properly applied, is a valuable one. After a desultory sort of survey—sufficiently minute, however, to take in all the requisite features of the new country—numbers of this class of adventurers followed their more excitable and erratic gold-digging fellows to the South. Here the story of the new land was told—the old days of high interests on advances, and of large commissions on agencies, remembered by the monied ones of the cities of the South with regret, and it was not difficult to persuade them to enter into similar ventures away up in the hot North. Within a couple of years stations had been taken up in all directions, up and down the coast-line of the country. Stock was carried to the new settlements by every possible means. The mere spending of the money requisite to carry out the plans of the day was a pleasant operation. Those who had borrowed the means to make a fresh start in life were perhaps the happiest of any; but the "new chums" who had brought money with them had a merry time of it also. It was a gay enough life, that seeking "pastures new" by the banks of beautiful rivers, on the pleasant plains, and the still more pleasant hill-sides. The work of exploring on and near the coast was light compared with that experienced by the pioneers on the Blue Mountains of New South Wales. That there were mountain ranges was true, here and there a deep river to cross, and not unfrequently a boggy or swampy track to be wandered round. The general features of the country more than compensated for these things, however. The swamps and bogs were rich in feed for cattle and sheep, and every lagoon and river-bend presented special beauties and attractions. The earliest settlement, almost as a matter of course, took place on or near the coast, though there were not wanting adventurers who ventured out towards the westward. Among these were many who travelled from Victoria overland, with sheep, for the purpose of stocking the Northern territory. Among these were to be found men of a class that is never likely to die out in the Australian colonies. Squatting is everywhere looked upon as quite an aristocratic pursuit when compared with the ordinary routine of trade, agriculture, or commerce, and numbers of persons engaged in business, after having grown rich, are especially desirous of being enrolled among the roll of the members of the "squattocracy." Many of these had, at the time referred to, made and saved money, and from time to time parties of such were formed for the purpose of taking up the new country in the North. Of course, they were as a rule totally inexperienced in the work pertaining to such pursuits, and failure was not an unfrequent result of the adventures. It would have been more wonderful still had success, under most of the circumstances, attended the endeavour. The initial step, the mere purchase of sheep and cattle, was surrounded with difficulties. Men whose whole lives had been devoted to the buying and selling of brandy, or gin, or sugar, or calico, or the manufacture of slops, or millinery, could hardly be expected to be fully competent to select for themselves and partners precisely the right kind of stock on the most favourable terms. That in many cases this was not done may be taken for granted. Then again, once the novelty of the affair having worn off, the long and wearisome journey was sufficient, save in the case of the young, strong, and unusually hopeful, to induce disaster and loss. At first, the journeying had all the charms of novelty. The short and easily performed stages of four, five, six, or ten miles a day left plenty of time for amusement, which too often took the shape of castle-building as to the golden fleeces they were to shear as the result of their labours. With the passing away of the months—many of such journeys occupied a year—the enjoyments of day and night dreaming, of 'possum and wild-duck shooting, began to pall. Some of the country was hard to travel over, and had to be crossed quickly, for the sake of the pasturage and water beyond. Pleasant vales and shady river-banks were not always met with on the journey. Long stretches of arid plain had to be traversed, now and then the natives became troublesome, cattle would stray, and the dingo make free with the sheep, and so time and patience were both sometimes lost. Arrived at the "Plains of Promise," the promises were not always fulfilled. Here and there, there stretched a belt of "poison country," luxuriant with a pleasant-looking pasturage, every leaf and blade of which carried death among the flocks and herds. Shearing-time, of which the new-fashioned squatters, in their urban innocence, had drawn pleasant pastoral pictures, and in their mercantile minds had totaled up large cash balances derivable therefrom, brought its own disappointments. Instead of the well-to-do squatter surveying his fleecy flock being passed through the patent dip or plunged in the clear waters of a running stream, the pasturers saw in each other only squalid men performing work of a hard and disagreeable character, and often began to regard the whole affair with disgust long before the first bales of wool were packed and dispatched towards the coast. "Dispatched *towards* the coast" is written advisedly, for, in numerous instances, the ill-clipped, worse packed, greasy wool never reached its destination until it had passed into other and more experienced hands. As a rule, this was the case with the flocks and herds and other belongings of the class of adventurers described, who, by the end of their second season of squatting, were glad to relinquish the novel and fascinating pursuit.

All these things notwithstanding, the experiences of the time were not of an entirely unprofitable or uninteresting character, and, for a season, success seemed certain to those who had brought capital and experience to bear on the experiment. As settlements increased, townships that had hitherto been such in name merely, assumed an importance and prospered beyond the wildest dreams of their first inhabitants. Then came other influences to bear. As early as 1854 cotton had been grown in and exported from the Moreton Bay district, and attention was naturally directed towards it and other products of tropical and semi-tropical countries. Then commenced the "mad season," that every English colony appears to pass through at one time or another of its career. The discovery, or rather the re-discovery, of gold in payable quantities tended to increase the excitement. The more the pasture countries up towards the Gulf of Carpentaria were explored, the more valuable they promised to be. The East coast rivers had many of their banks taken up for other than squatting purposes. The pursuits of cotton and sugar-growing were largely entered into. The usual "land rackit" took place. Building allotments in the towns, and farms in the bush, were eagerly sought after, and the former purchased at high prices. The new industries prospered beyond expectation, and the most glowing anticipations were indulged in by all manner of men. The old squatters grew richer than even their hopes had comprehended. The new **arrivals** who had brought money into the colony with them would **only be contented** with beginning their race of life, as young married **people do everywhere nowadays, in a fashion far more extravagant than their elders indulged in after** their **fortunes had** been **made.** Everything was **rose-coloured. Horses, sheep, and** cattle multiplied exceedingly. **Geological research indicated that the metal-bearing** properties of the country were very great, **and these indications were** justified by after-experiences. The raising of sugar proved a profitable investment, whilst the farming operations proper carried on on the Darling Downs, and other places situate high above the sea-level, were successful to a degree that the firmest believer in the colony had never expected. For a time, all "went merry as a marriage bell." Most glowing accounts of the prosperity were sent to the people-bearing colonies and to England, and these attracted men with money, more or less, and the most brilliant hopes for the future were entertained by **every one.**

There was one drawback to the general contentment, however. Labouring men were scarce, and those in the colony commanded high pay. This fact detracted somewhat from the profits, position, and anticipations of the squatter, the cotton and sugar grower, as well as the ordinary farmer and trader. These people could absorb far more than all the available labour in the colony, and, in order to keep pace with the rapid advance of things, it was absolutely necessary that certain projected public works should be carried out. Railways had to be made, or ordinary roads improved, rivers bridged, and telegraph-lines constructed. The situation was perplexing, and the wise men and law-makers of the colony put their **heads together** and decided on adopting the old fallacy of "systematic **emigration."** The natural flow of population towards a more than usually prosperous country failed to meet the circumstances of the case, so money was voted and steps at once taken to secure a supply of the coveted commodity.

The land laws of the colony were adapted to meet the requirements of men with small means, and a, by no means under-coloured, programme of the advantages offered prepared. Provided with these as credentials, a gentleman was appointed at a handsome salary to proceed to England and proclaim Queensland as the promised land. The text was an excellent one, and the discourse was almost equal to it. The time was singularly propitious also. The prosperity that had characterized the position of a certain proportion of the working classes, in consequence of the American War, was more than counterbalanced by the terrible sufferings of those whose means of living had been taken away by the same disaster. Mail after mail had brought to the Australian colonies news of the want and misery experienced by the cotton workers in Lancashire, and right nobly did the Australians respond to the appeal, "Con yo help uz a bit?" Every colony contributed money to the Lancashire Relief Fund, but Queensland could do more. It could send cotton also. Here was an irresistible argument. Every one who chose to emigrate could become a landowner, and, by his labour, assist in the production of cotton, and thus enable the dear ones at home to continue the employment to which they had all their lives been accustomed. The glorious climate—for, the heat notwithstanding, the climate of Queensland is a glorious one—the beautiful scenery, the strange forms of vegetable life, the luxuriance of the land, every advantage most to be desired by men upon whose fortunes evil days had fallen, were told of in glowing colours, and with an almost poetic imagery. Nor was this all. The independence to be secured, the happy lives to be led, the congenial employments to be engaged in, and the great future of the colony and its colonists, were dwelt upon by the lecturer and agent with a fervour admirably calculated to convince people of his truthfulness. Add to this that the people were desirous of being convinced, more than this indeed, that, in innumerable instances, any change they could make must have appeared to be for the better, and the success of the "systematic emigration," so far as the deportations of people went, was secured.

It was a motley mustering of people that was gathered together week after week, and month after month, by the exertions of the agent. Of course, out of the hundreds and thousands who elected to go and partake of the advantages offered them, were many admirably calculated and adapted for the work of colonisation they had undertaken. Wherever English men and women gather together, such men and women will not be wanting. They are first of all blessed with health and strength, and the courage that can encounter difficulties bravely and hopefully. More than this, they possess the faculty of adapting themselves to the various circumstances of life. Of such men it has been said "they can bore a hole with a hand-saw, and saw a plank with a gimblet;" and of such women, that they can sacrifice everything of comfort and ease, face difficulty and overcome it, under any and every circumstance, when the welfare of those to whom they are attached is involved. Of course such people would succeed anywhere, and to the fact that there were many of these is attributable whatever of success attended the experiment under notice. Men and women of this stamp formed, however, a very small proportion of those who availed themselves of the opportunity to emigrate afforded them. On the contrary, general unfitness for a life of endurance under strange circumstances was the chief characteristic of the majority of those who left their homes in search of a new life in a new land. The Lancashire cotton weaver, who had all his life been used to his regular work during regular hours, whose existence had been, for the most part, a sedentary and a mechanical one, was "all abroad" on the sugar or cotton fields of the coast lands of Queensland. When he sought the ordinary labour he was, if possible, still more at sea. The perpetually varying occupations of a farmer's life within the tropic of Capricorn proved to be a burden impossible to bear. Many of this class were soon sickened of the way of life into which they had fallen; and in seeking other means of living they fell into a still worse case. There were others equally unfortunate and equally unfitted for the routine of the new life upon which they had entered. These were young men, some of them having received first-class educations qualifying them for professions, clerks, shopmen, nondescripts, and ne'er-do-weels, who had sought Queensland with vague hopes of fortune-making by some means or other, but, as a rule, as utterly useless for colonial purposes as it was well possible for men to be. Of course these people were all bitterly disappointed; and equally of course they laid the whole blame of their misfortunes upon the colony and **upon those** who had misrepresented it. Sad stories of suffering and disaster were told, **and** many of them had firm foundation in facts. Still the **stream** of systematic emigration continued, for favourable circumstances still continued **at home,** and the same rose-coloured representations continued to be made. **Not** unnaturally the end came sooner than had been expected, but the result was by no means all evil. In common with many of those who joined in the first "mad rush" to Port Curtis, there were some among the "systematized" ones who determined to make the best of what they considered to be a bad job, plucked up courage and went to work with a will. Nearly every man endowed with this feeling prospered, and to-day some of the richest and most prosperous farmers and traders of Queensland can trace their success to the hard work and training that resulted from their first failures in the colony. That the neighbouring colonies, New South Wales and Victoria at any rate, and probably New Zealand, benefited very considerably by the circumstances that tended to make the emigrants discontented with Queensland cannot be doubted. Thousands of men and women who had been introduced from the United Kingdom at the expense of the Government, found their way from Queensland, at small expense to themselves, and thus aided in enriching the Southern colonies.

The imported labourers, mechanics, clerks, and adventurers of various designations, were not the only people who met with disappointment in Queensland. As has already been shown, squatting pursuits had been entered into by persons wholly unaccustomed to and unfitted for the life, and failure had been the result. The persistent painting of prosperous prospects indulged in by lecturers and others, had had the effect of attracting large numbers of young men from the mother country and the elder colonies. Very many of these brought money, varying in amount from a few hundreds to a few thousand pounds each. Full of life, and hope, and vigour, they entered into the operation of obtaining "colonial experience" with a zest and unwisdom that very soon told its own tale upon their fortunes. Many of these men with some £5,000 to the good had no hesitation in incurring obligations to the extent of some five or six times the money possessed by themselves. There was no lack of merchants and moneyed agents content, if not anxious, to assist them in carrying out their arrangements. Thus owners of large stations were to be found in various directions, the only result of whose operations was the absorption of their original capital into the pockets of the agents who had at first assisted them in their career. These agents, of course, held the security of the whole property for the assistance they had rendered; and when the process of absorption was complete, there was only one result possible. The squatter had notice to quit, or possibly became manager of the station of which he had fondly hoped to be the owner for ever. All these various circumstances culminated in something very like a crash, and the few years of unhealthy excitement and unsound prosperity was succeeded by a season of depression and loss. Nearly every interest in the colony was unfavourably affected. Squatters mourned over the "good old times" of less than half-a-score of years before. Only for frequently recurring gold discoveries, a very low state of affairs might have been reached. As it was, trade became dull, and there was a general break-up and a partial clearing out. Properties were sacrificed, and valuable interests abandoned; but the end was not yet.

The inherent value of the country and pluck of the people soon asserted themselves. During the worst of the bad times public works were continued, and those who were content to plod on did not do so very badly after all. During the years referred to, the Queenslanders had held their first great Exhibition, and they have held one such every year since. With what interest such an affair could be surrounded, those who visited the Queensland annexe at the International Exhibition at South Kensington in 1873-74, under the management of the Agent-General, Mr. Daintree, can easily understand. In 1864 the colony was visited by most disastrous floods, and this calamity added to the other influences of misfortune. By 1865 the first railway had been opened, and in the previous year telegraphic communication had been carried as far north as Rockhampton; and eight years later the same element of civilisation and progress was completed to the shores of the Gulf of Carpentaria. Thus the colony not only overcame the difficulties almost universally attendant upon first efforts, but laid the foundations of a prosperity of no mean magnitude. Towns had been founded, municipal and borough institutions established, churches and school-houses built by the score. Railways had been carried across mountain-ranges and over valleys, and new districts of country thus opened up. Taught wisdom by the mistakes of the past, the Government, whilst continuing to pay, and pay heavily, for emigration, exercises, through the agency of its Agent-General already referred to, a wise discretion in the mode of conducting that department of business. New industries are constantly springing up. Farms and homesteads abound in every direction. The squatter has flourished in spite of the free selecters, and both have discovered not only that their interests need not be antagonistic, but that each can benefit the other. The cultivation of sugar has become one of the most profitable pursuits, and, by the adoption of certain practices of manufacture, can be engaged in by any one. Cotton and coffee can be profitably cultivated; the trees of the colony are being profitably utilised for industrial purposes. The waters of the bays, rivers, and sea yield their harvests also; hundreds of plants and shrubs valuable for medicinal and other purposes are attracting attention, and the future of Queensland promises to be a prosperous one. Cotton, if not quite so important, is still a steadily growing interest.

THE TIN DISCOVERIES. 175

Gold-fields have been and are still being profitably worked in various localities from the extreme south to the extreme north of the colony. Coal, iron, and copper abound; whilst precious stones, diamonds, rubies, opals, are by no means rare. Tin has been discovered and worked to an extent that has considerably affected the market of that mineral in England. One circumstance in relation to this is worth relating. The tin of commerce is described as numbers one, two, and three, the first-named taking first place as to quality. Soon after the introduction of Queensland tin to the English market, it was remarked that the lower qualities totally disappeared. For a long time a mystery surrounded the circumstance, but at length it was discovered that the Australian tin was of so pure a quality that **the Cornish smelters had been enabled,** by mixing it with the two lower qualities of English and Straits tin, **to** raise the standard of their entire stock up to the level of first-class metal. This was done, and large sums of money were said to have been realised by the practice. Added to these things must be taken the fact that population has steadily increased, and bids fair to continue to do so; that every year brings to light fresh discoveries of land suitable for settlement; that meat-preserving and wine-making have become valuable industries; that, with **a knowledge of the** climate, a habit of adaptability has been adopted by the **people, and** so **the** secret of success is made plain. The question **of Coolie labour is** hardly one to be treated of here. Under proper management there **is** no reason why it should not be profitably employed, and evidence is in favour of the kindly treatment accorded to the coloured labourer by the Queensland employer. It is, however, a vexed question, the solution of which must be left to time and experience.

The various indications of the prosperity referred to will be more conveniently described in the succeeding pages, as the several features of the country are brought under review.

CHAPTER XIX

QUEENSLAND—*continued*.

EXTENT OF QUEENSLAND.—THE COAST COUNTRY.—ENTERING THE COLONY.—THE TIN-PRODUCING DISTRICT.—WARWICK.—TOOWOOMBA.—THE DARLING DOWNS.—WANT OF APPRECIATION.—WHEAT GROWING.—OASIS.—THE INTERIOR EXPLORERS.

This colony, the brief history of **which has been** thus briefly sketched, from its very extent, presents varied characteristics of natural features. Extending as it does from 29° S. to 10° S., and from 138° to 153° E., it includes an area of land nearly a dozen times as large as England, its acreage being reckoned at about 440,000,000. That it contains within this area a great variety of soils, **and** experiences some variations of climate, can be easily understood. The lands best adapted for agriculture are nearly all to be found within **one hundred and fifty miles** of the **Pacific coast**. In common with **New South Wales and Victoria, Queensland has a long** stretch of mountain ranges running parallel with the **sea-line**. Sometimes these hills approach within twenty or twenty-five miles of the waters of the **Pacific**, this peculiarity being chiefly apparent at the extreme north and the extreme **south** of the colony. The eastern coast line can hardly measure less **than 2,000** miles, and, of course, includes many bays and promontories. The **Coast** Range is little, if anything, short of this length. As though Nature **had** intended to do her best for the colony, the broadest belt of land adapted **for** agricultural purposes exists close upon its southern boundary. This district is known as the Darling Downs, and to this tract of country a more extended notice will be given by-and-by.

Bidding defiance to the obstacles presented by the Macpherson Range—the natural boundary between Queensland and New South Wales—we will, for the sake of convenience and brevity, enter the former colony at the point where we left the latter, and run away west from Point Danger some fifty miles or so. Such a journey would be a difficult, almost an impossible, one; but when achieved, at the end of it the traveller would find himself on or near the most southerly gold-field of Queensland. More than this he would be a very short **distance** from the tin mines, that promise to be almost as valuable **as** those yielding gold, or copper, or coal. Stanthorpe the tin town is called, **and it would** be difficult to find a more picturesque country than that surrounding it. The westerly-running range round about here breaks up into comparatively low-lying points and peaks, with narrow valleys between each. These hills and valleys present varied features of natural beauty. The hill tops and sides present features queer and quaint, for the boulders and rocks appear to have been thrown together with a view simply to the picturesque, united with the strange and out-of-the-way. The valleys are, nearly all of them, eminently calculated for pleasant homesteads to be set into pleasant frameworks of hills and ranges. When the time comes—and come it surely will, and that before long—when the rainfall of these regions shall be conserved, then will every one of those valleys be abiding-places for happy and prosperous people. **Stanthorpe has sprung up since** the discovery of the tin deposits, and is, as **is nearly every other mining township, built without** any attempt at regularity, and **of such materials—wood, or bark, or iron—as** were found most convenient and come-at-able. It is a prosperous place, and when the tin-mining industry becomes better defined and more developed, its **prosperity** is sure to increase. A good deal of the country round about is **admirably** adapted for settlement, and, as gold and coal are to be found not far away, the miners and others connected with mining are sure to avail themselves of all the facilities for settlement the district may afford them. Already the town possesses a hospital, and the Good Templars have erected a hall in which to teach the desirability of temperance. The Church of England, the Roman Catholics, Wesleyans, and Presbyterians have all got places of worship in the town; whilst, as a matter of course, the banking and spirit-selling interests are well represented. Some thirty miles nearly due north of Stanthorpe lies a town of which Southern Queenslanders are not **a little** proud. It bears the name of the great king-maker of England, and if the people who live thereabouts are to be depended upon, or their judgment trusted—and there is little, if any, reason to doubt either—Warwick **will,** by-and-by, be the king of towns in that part of the world. Brisbane, a hundred miles away, may boast of its harbour, and of its being the seat of government; Ipswich, somewhat nearer to hand, may have its river-frontages and its possibilities of sugar growing: but Warwick, say the Warwickers, has the grand Darling Downs as its backbone and spinal marrow, with tin, and gold, and coal, and diamonds, and amethysts, and a delicious climate, beautiful scenery, and a river second to none in the broad colony, as ribs radiating therefrom; and, therefore, it must some day attain and retain the first place in Queensland. Whether these anticipations be fulfilled or no, certain it is that the Warwick of 1875 is a thoroughly **well-**to-do and prosperous town. As is common in Australia, the streets are broad and handsome, and laid out at right angles with each other. Most people think the town pretty; so it is; but Mr. Anthony Trollope, on his first visit to Australia—bearing with him, of course, long-fixed notions of old cathedral towns, with their narrow and inconvenient streets, their picturesque buildings, genteel closes, and solemn cloisters—thought otherwise. He conceived the place "parallelogrammic and monotonous, the mountains too far away to give it any attraction, and the river sluggish." In short he looked upon its being ugly as "a necessity of its condition." Subsequent visits will doubtless remove this impression. Whether this may be the case or no does not much matter. The climate of Warwick is unsurpassed for salubrity, the lands surrounding it highly fertile; the river Condamine, a pleasant enough stream in certain seasons, by no means deserving the character of sluggish given it by Mr. Trollope. The streets, to which he took objection because of rectangularity, measure fifty miles in length, and though open spaces occur here and there they are rapidly filling up. Warwick manages to support, and very creditably too, a brace of newspapers sufficiently opposed to each other on local subjects and general politics to give a zest to the writings they contain, and to ensure the interest of the town and district being looked after in an onerous manner.

Although Warwick claims and obtains considerable riches from its contiguity to the now-celebrated Darling Downs, there is another town, Toowoomba, lying to the north of it, that is, in reality, the capital of that famous district. Toowoomba is situate on the summit of the range of mountains that divides what, in government-surveying parlance, is called the settled from the unsettled districts of Queensland. It may be as well to say here that these terms, settled and unsettled, explain only in degree the districts referred to, for both are more or less settled. In the settled districts,—that is to say, a strip of country running the entire length of the colony along the coast, and extending westward from perhaps twenty to two hundred miles,—the free selector, as distinguished from the squatter, is master of the situation. Up to a certain and very considerable extent, he can, on this line of seaboard, and on the plateaus with which many of the mountains are crowned, select on very favourable terms land sufficient for all the ordinary purposes of farming. By fulfilling certain easy conditions and making certain very easy payments, the land so selected becomes the property of the selecter, and remains at the absolute disposal of himself, "his heirs, executors, and assigns" for ever. Being thus situated, Toowoomba enjoys an exceptionally favourable position. It is nearly two thousand feet above the sea level, and possesses a climate as nearly resembling that of Madeira as possible. It is, as indeed most towns in the colony are, a municipality, and contains rather more than the ordinary average of public buildings, including churches and chapels, banks, hotels, and stores. The School of Arts at Toowoomba would be considered a creditable institution in many towns of far larger pretensions. The library connected with it has been judiciously selected, and its advantages are well appreciated by the inhabitants. The hospital is a more than creditable erection, and its affairs are administered in a manner that gives satisfaction at once to its subscribers and the recipients of its bounty. What with its constantly growing agricultural industries, the already established mines in its neighbourhood, and its other varied advantages, there is little to wonder at in this model Australian town being highly thought of by its inhabitants, and it would require the adverse judgment of a good many flying visitors to unfix their faith in that particular. As an evidence of its growing prosperity may be taken the fact that in the month of December, 1874, the money receipts of the Toowoomba Land Office exceeded £16,000.

For fully forty years after the discovery of the Darling Downs by the botanist Allan Cunningham, in 1827, these widespreading table-lands were looked upon as a feeding-place for flocks and herds only. Since the "seventies" came in a change has been brought about. As in Victoria and New South Wales, so in Queensland. The pastoral tenants of the Crown failed to understand that anything better than the natural pasturage of the country could be raised in it, so that when the idea of cultivating the ground was first mooted, it was hard to say whether the feeling of wonder or contempt was uppermost. With the opening up of the tin mines and the adjustment of the land laws, both these feelings were modified. Fencing and ploughing, and sowing, and reaping, and mowing, were hard facts to controvert, and when the two last-named operations became realised with profitable results the squatters, like sensible men, came to understand that they must accept the inevitable. It is hardly to be wondered at that squatters should be difficult to convince of the wisdom of a mode of procedure that appears to militate against their own immediate interests; but that intelligent visitors, such as Mr. Trollope for instance, with, as may be taken for granted, no personal bias either way, should believe or propagate an error that has been exploded over and over again in Australia, is a matter to grieve at somewhat. Speaking of the Darling Downs, he tells the world that "wheat has been produced, but not so as to pay the grower of it;" and again, "the Queensland farmer cannot produce wheat." The farmers of the Darling Downs have proved both these statements to be erroneous. They have grown wheat, they are growing wheat, and they will grow more of it in future, and they have derived a profit as the result of their operations.

From Toowoomba the railroad runs right through the Darling Downs to Dalby, a town sure to rise in importance with the growing industries of the colony. It would be difficult to equal for pleasant prospects and interesting outlines the railway ride of some fifty miles or so between Dalby and Toowoomba. Save the vast expanse of the country passed through, there is nothing of the grand or majestic in the scenery, but it possesses charms that can never fail to please. The term "Down" fails to convey a very distinct idea of the character of the country. The long stretches of the South Downs of England, indeed, fail entirely in this respect. Before the idiotic potentate who raised the absurd and colossal mound near Hougoumont destroyed the natural features of the country, the field of Waterloo must have presented a strong resemblance to many portions of the Darling Downs of Queensland. The surface undulates considerably; here and there pleasant-looking and valuable watercourses carry fertility and beauty to the lands bounding them. At somewhat long distances apart, the vast volcanic table-land is broken by upheaved mounts of granite or sandstone. These hills are of no great height, but they add variety to the landscape, and it is impossible to imagine anything more picturesque than are many of the valleys with which these elevations are every now and then intersected. The hill-sides are all, or nearly all, timbered with a vast variety of trees and shrubs, the foliage and flowers of which serve as a most pleasing foil to the level lands by which they are surrounded. Springs exist of course on the mountain-sides, and these, as their waters find their way to the plains below, add an element of beauty to the scene that only the traveller coming from the vast plains and deserts of the West can properly appreciate. How cool and pleasant they look, and how soothing is the sound of their waters as they find their way in and out and round about the shady trees and unexpected points of the hills! To one coming from "a dry and thirsty land," these little Edens possess a peculiar and never-to-be-forgotten charm, and now new homes and villages are adding their attractions to the other characteristics of the place. The natural pasturage of the Downs is of a rich and varied character, and in no part of the world, perhaps, could a greater number of different grasses, and herbs, and roots be gathered within a given space.

West and north of Dalby lie the vast unsettled districts of Queensland.

AN AUSTRALIAN EXHIBITION. 181

That the term "unsettled" is somewhat of a misnomer has been already intimated. For the first few miles farms are met with, and then come the vast and apparently unending plains upon which men are scarce enough, but sheep and oxen plentiful. The farms referred to, and the farmers occupying them, have by no means allowed their energies to be cramped by their close proximity to their squatting neighbours. This has, within the last twelve years, dating from 1863, been evidenced by the excellence of the agricultural and other produce exhibited at the Exhibitions of Draytown and Toowoomba, held in the year 1875 for the twelfth time. Some of the wines were pronounced of unusual excellence. Prizes were adjudged for horses, comprising those best calculated for farming purposes, blood brood-mares adapted for quick travelling or racing, steady-going hackneys and harness horses, whilst colts and fillies were well represented. Cattle was, of course, well to the fore, and so were pigs and poultry. All these are comparatively commonplace in Australia, and in these things Queensland partakes of the common character of the other colonies in raising everything of the best kind attainable, and some of the best stock of England, or their immediate progeny, has been imported into Queensland. The Toowoomba exhibits include other things, however. Ploughs, and rakes, and harrows of the best possible kind are exhibited and appreciated; whilst such "small deer" as potatoes, cabbages, beans, peas, carrots, cauliflowers, parsnips, cucumbers, pumpkins, melons, tobacco, olive oil, and opium serve to swell the list. Fruit is, of course, an important item, and those who grow peaches in hot-houses in England at the rate of a shilling each, would be delighted to see the delicate fruits of the Darling Downs grown in the open air.

This is somewhat of a digression, but no journey made across the Downs would have served the most ordinary purposes of travel without observation being directed to these things; and having thus just glanced at them, the most convenient way of noting the chief objects of interest will be to strike a bee line for six hundred miles or so due west from Dalby. Very much of the country thus indicated would be simply impassable, save by a bird, and every here and there such a traveller would often require to make a long day's journey, perhaps several, from one waterhole, or creek, or river, to another. The route would not be without its interest, however, and, as being the most convenient mode of describing this part of the country, it is adopted. Starting, then, from a point that may, for all practicable purposes, be described as 27° south, and 151° east, the journeyer towards the west would at first, and for a hundred miles or so, pass through a well-watered and comparatively luxuriant country. His course would be north of a spur of the dividing range, and for a very considerable distance, pretty nearly parallel with that of the Condamine River. Leaving the Darling district, he would enter that of Maranoa. Here he would find vast salt-bush plains, these forming a thoroughly good grazing country. The high lands between the few and far between creeks are almost without exception composed of long stretches of sandy soil, utterly valueless for any other purpose save that of receiving rainfall, and, by the various watercourses, passing it on to the salt-bush country upon which the sheep feed. There are several townships in the district of Maranoa, but none of them calling for any special mention. Whilst crossing this district, the tracks of several of the men who first opened up the *terra incognita* of Australia would be met with, and, in connection with every one of them, tales of the deepest interest have been told. They equal, if not surpass, any tales of heroic endurance and sublime effort with which the world has been made acquainted. This is not the place, however, in which to repeat them, but at some future time the tales may, with great propriety, be perfected and told over again. On the east side of Maranoa, and somewhat to the south of the spurs of the coast range, the track followed by Kennedy the explorer, in 1847, would be crossed. Towards the western extremity of Maranoa, a low-lying country, wooded with scrub, many of the belts of timber of which attain the dignity of forests, extends southward to the boundary of New South Wales. Passing into the Warrego district, the country continues to maintain its character. Plains fit for pasturage, belts of scrub, long reaches of valueless desert, low-lying hills, watercourses often dry, though sometimes subject to floods, alternate with each other. On one of the creeks well up towards the western boundary, Dr Becker, a most enthusiastic explorer and botanist, found a resting-place. Passing over the Booboo, for so the creek is called, a solitary mountain, called by the same name, stands out sheer and distinct from the surrounding arid land. Soon after this landmark is passed, the track of the explorers, Robert O'Hara Burke, John Wills, and John King is met with, and a hundred miles or so farther west Cooper's Creek, where Burke and Wills died. The country for some—indeed, hundreds—of miles round about here is rich in memorials of the men who at the risk and often the loss of life, by unwearied patience opened up what was indeed and in truth a new world. A quarter of a century ago, a vast blank on the map of Australia was the chief record of the interior. Not far away—long distances become small when compared with the extent of the country—both Sturt and Stuart fought a gallant fight against the hard, waterless, rocky desert. Time after time they, and Gregory, Mitchell, McKinley, and others, pierced the sterile, rocky barrier by which the country on every side appeared to be bounded, and made their way to green spots, where they rested, and after rest renewed their efforts, only to be defeated however. Leichardt, one of the first, if not the very first, of those who laid down their life in the cause of exploration, has left a record of his labours in the name of a creek; and, indeed, some such memorial remains of most of those who have engaged in the work of discovery.

That the result of the labours of these men was of a more practical character than this every reader knows. Stretches of good land were found to intersect the desert, and upon these the squatter feeds his flocks and herds and grows rich. The work of discovery continues from month to month, and, indeed, from day to day. The stock-rider and intending settler leave few nooks or corners unexamined, and every piece of pastoral country they discover and utilise is one more tribute to the courage and abnegation of self they have manifested in their lives. The following memorial lines were written when the news of Robert O'Hara Burke's death was received; and, though they but feebly convey the feelings of the writer and of those who knew the explorer, may be accepted as indicating the excellencies of many who unsuccessfully preceded him and of others who have since followed in his footsteps, successfully, because of his example and the teachings of his endeavour, his triumph, and his death :—

"Awakened from the dream of life," O friend !
We weep, with more than friendship, o'er thy grave.
Yet, whilst we mourn thee, our departed brave,
Best of all comfort with our grief doth blend.
Better be such an one as thou art, dead,
Than half a world of common living men.
True soul, brave heart, and gentlest gentle-man,
Strong soul and hand to work and brain to plan,
"We ne'er may look upon thy like again ;"
Yet o'er thy memory such rich love is shed
As lifts thee far above men's praise or blame—
It casts a halo round thy ended time,
And gilds with perfect reverence thy name,
Making thy lonely death a life sublime.

CHAPTER XX.

QUEENSLAND

A NARROW-GAUGE RAILWAY.—A TRAIN BLOWN OVER.—A WINDING JOURNEY.—
IPSWICH.—THE GOOD OLD TIMES.—THE BRISBANE RIVER AND ITS SETTLE-
MENTS.—DOWN THE RIVER.—BRISBANE.—THE BOTANIC GARDENS.—THEIR
CURATOR.—TREES, BEES, FISH.

TURNING away from the interior of Australia, and travelling towards Brisbane on the east, the track already passed over will of course have to be retraced for some distance. Crossing, therefore, the desert patches, the fertile plains, the luxuriant downs and welcome watercourses, we next, in order to give some system to the description of the colony, strike the **railway at** Toowoomba once more. We would, indeed, strike a junction **of railways, for the southern** extension of the main line here takes its **way towards Warwick, of which** town something has been told in the previous chapter. **This railway** is notable on several accounts. Not only has it helped to open up valuable districts of the colony, but it has also added to the stability thereof. There are several peculiarities pertaining to it worth noticing. First of all its gauge is of the narrowest, consequently the engines and carriages that run upon it are upon a small scale; so small, indeed, as to be sometimes termed toy-like. Nevertheless they do good work, and both gauge and carriages were adopted at a time when it would have been next to impossible to adopt a wider gauge or a heavier and more impressive style of rolling stock. It was "a day of small things" when the railways from Ipswich to Toowoomba and Dalby on the west, and towards Warwick on the south were commenced, and Queenslanders were wisely frugal. That the term "toy-like" is not wholly inappropriate may be gathered from the circumstance that one day early in 1875 a high wind swept over and across the hills, and meeting a train on its course lifted several of the carriages bodily off the rails, depositing them quietly **on** the roadside, and fortunately at a spot where the banks of the line ran nearly level. One of the most famous judges of Australia, Sir **Redmond Barry,** of **Victoria, was a** passenger by the train, but luckily sustained **no injury. Perhaps** by way of impressing the lessons derivable from railway accidents, one of the four of those injured on the occasion was the mayor of Warwick, to which town the train was proceeding.

As may easily be **imagined** from what has been already **said respecting**

A PANORAMA.   185

the natural features of the **hill country of** the east coast of Australia, the **passage** through the coast **range from** Toowoomba to Ipswich is of an **interesting** and highly picturesque character. The railway winds round **about** the ranges in quite a different fashion to that pursued by the line crossing the Blue Mountains from Sydney to Bathurst. There is very little of the "going right ahead" principle on the western railway of Queensland. It **turns** and twists in a fashion that some people have described as erratic, but it shows method in the apparent madness. Tunnels are cunningly placed, and gradients fixed. Often the route travelled would seem to carry the journeyer in directly the opposite direction to that in which **he desires** to go; but after passing crags and peaks innumerable, some **hanging, as** it were, in mid-air above, and others **frowning in** the **gorges below, the** level of the river is reached, **and soon afterwards the town of Ipswich** itself entered.

Although, for the sake of keeping the description of the country as compact in form as possible, the railway journey over the dividing range has been made from west to east, the traveller in search of the more salient points of natural beauty would do well to reverse the route, and travel from the coast towards the hills and the plains beyond. With railways, as with most other things, moral and physical, coming down the hill is, when compared with the process of going up it, a rapid one. Although the **same** scenes are passed on the downward as on the upward journey, the **latter** affords more time for investigation and contemplation than the **former,** and therefore it is recommended. There is much to **repay the slow** passenger on his westward course on the railway referred to. **He passes** a panorama of ever-varying beauty. Quiet and peaceful valleys **alternate** with rugged peaks and rocks, whilst the vistas of views obtainable **through** some of the openings in the hills are of exceeding beauty, **and in not a few** instances, of sublimity.

Like many a good old roadside town in the **good** old coaching **days in** England, Ipswich has suffered somewhat, after a certain fashion, from **the** opening of the railways **to** the west and south. Before the steam horse **had** found **its way over the hills,** Ipswich was the grand depôt for the **reception of wool and other produce** from the Darling Downs, and of the **stores necessary for station life, from** Brisbane. The Bremer, a branch **of the Brisbane river, was the "silent** highway" by which the traffic between **Ipswich and the coast was** carried on. During the season **bullock-drays used to arrive in scores and** hundreds from the west, and **steamers nearly**

3 B

every day from Brisbane. The town was full of life and activity. People made money enough in a month or so to carry them on for a year. Of course with the opening of the railway came the doing away with, to a considerable extent, the bullock-drays and horse-teams. By-and-by, when the extension of the railway from Brisbane to Ipswich is effected, the traffic with the interior will go right through without change of conveyance, and one of the sources of the importance of Ipswich will have departed. It has many things to fall back upon, however, and its career is a prosperously progressive one. It is somewhat more irregularly built than is the case with most Australian towns; but this very irregularity imparts to it a picturesque aspect that right-angled streets are said to lack. The position of the town is a favourable one in nearly every respect. It occupies the slopes of the gently rising hills, down the side of which the drainage is naturally conveyed into the river Bremer. Many of the public buildings, including an endowed school, as well as the mercantile establishments, are exceedingly handsome. Churches and chapels abound as a matter of course, whilst a public library and school of art afford amusement and instruction of an intellectual sort. The trade of the town is considerable. Coal mines have been worked in its neighbourhood for several years, whilst the area of ground devoted to agriculture is being added to rapidly. There are fully twenty thousand acres of land under cultivation, the chief crops being maize and cotton, both of which grow most luxuriantly, and the culture of them is consequently very profitable. The town proper contains a population of about seven thousand; that of the district being fully ten thousand. Within the boundaries of the municipality there are over thirty miles of proclaimed roads and streets, and the property situate in and upon these roads is assessed, for rating purposes, at £500,000. Having these figures in view it is hardly to be wondered at that Ipswich claims to be the second town of southern Queensland; at one time, indeed, "first place or nowhere" was the motto of its then conservative inhabitants. "Trade and commerce," however, proved too strong for "pastoral pursuits," and Brisbane has gained thereby.

The journey from Ipswich to Brisbane, whether by road or river, is a pleasant one. Just where Ipswich is situate the river is somewhat narrow, but at various points on its way towards the sea it opens out into wide and long reaches that sometimes assume the appearance of by no means inconsiderable lakes. Although here and there there are patches of poor country on either side, the banks bounding the rivers Bremer and Brisbane—

for the former is a not inconsiderable or unimportant affluent of the latter—are, for agricultural purposes, of an exceedingly rich and valuable character. Nor have the natural advantages of the country been allowed to remain idle. Hard, intelligently pursued work has, within the last few years, altered very materially the appearance of both rivers. Corn, and cotton, and tobacco, abound hereabouts; and pleasant, prosperous, and comfortable houses are to be met with on every point and indentation. In places where the river narrows in, the shrubs and trees with which the banks are enriched assume a willow-like appearance that adds considerably to the quiet beauty of the scene. At these points the river runs rapidly, too rapidly indeed sometimes. In the March of 1875, after one of the heaviest rains ever experienced in the colony—nearly twelve inches of rain having fallen within twenty-four hours—the Bremer rose so rapidly and so high that the wharves were submerged and the goods sheds erected thereon swept bodily away. Such accidents as these, however, are not without an attendant good. Some day not far distant Australia will conserve the rainfall, and so turn to good account that which is now an evil of no inconsiderable magnitude.

Brisbane, bright, beautiful, busy Brisbane, will ere long be as great a source of pride to its inhabitants as Sydney has always been to the people of New South Wales. The feeling is quite justifiable, for the city possesses nearly everything necessary to commend itself to a high estimation in the minds of its residents. There are no very striking architectural features about the buildings, either public or private, of the city, but its natural surroundings fully make up for this. There is, perhaps, no town in Australia where more pleasant sites for pleasant homes exist than in and around Brisbane. The river, from the mouth of which it is situate some sixteen miles, winds round and indeed through the town, for, although bearing different names, Brisbane proper, South Brisbane, Fortitude Valley, and Kangaroo Point may all be fairly included in the one general term. In every direction pleasant homes are met with, and the gardens surrounding these are, almost without exception, worthy of the rich summer land in which they are placed. The mercantile community of Brisbane—and the whole community is more or less mercantile—exhibits a good deal of the friendly rivalry that exists among the merchant class everywhere, as to the appearance of the surroundings of their every-day life. The noble mansion, genteel villa, snug cottage, all find a place here. Shops, of course, abound; and they are for the most part gay as shops need be. The

188 AUSTRALIA ILLUSTRATED.

premises of the "————, ———, and others" are all handsome buildings ———————, ——— ———— and arranged for the purposes ——— ——— ———— —— ———. ——— various religious bodies have —— ——— ———— ———, ———, ——— schoolhouses. There is no ————— ——— ——— —————— have seven churches, the ————————— ————— —— ——— ——————, ——— Wesleyans and Congre-gational ————— ——— ———, ——— ——— —— ——— Catholics ———, including ——— Cathedral of St. Stephen, which although not completed, has been opened for public worship long ago. The Houses of Legislature were ——— ————, and so is the ————— ———————. News papers, ———— of institutes, schools of art, they are called in Australia, benevolent institu-tions, theatres, mutual improvement societies, and indeed all the appliances and surroundings of a high civilization, abound in Brisbane. That the people are equal to the external appearance of their city need hardly be told: they are bold, speculative, and enterprising. That they enjoy themselves thoroughly is a mere necessity of the climate and country in which they live, and they take advantage of their surroundings to the fullest extent.

The city of Brisbane is almost entirely surrounded by water. Thus it has, on every side, nearly all the ordinary attributes of natural beauty as to scenery and position. The town is to be found on both sides the surrounding water, and in order to connect the north with the south, an iron bridge, nearly a quarter of a mile in length, has been erected at a considerable cost. The commerce of the city is carried on by means of direct intercourse with the neighbouring colonies and the mother country. It has its own mail communication with England, the service of which is conducted efficiently and well. The route is by way of Torres Straits and Singapore, and since the commencement of the service the mails have, save in cases of rare accident, been delivered with admirable punctuality.

Among all the bright places about Brisbane the Botanic Garden is, perhaps, the brightest. This not simply because of its position and aspect, or of the pleasant uses to which it is put by the Brisbanites, but because also of its intrinsic value from an economic point of view. Perhaps there are no gardens in the world in which more important and interesting experi-ments in the acclimatization of plants have taken place than in those of Bris-bane. The feathery bamboos of Africa and Hindostan are to be found there, running straight up to a height of over seventy feet, their fronds forming a shade by no means to be slighted during the bright sunny afternoons of

Queensland. Poplars are plentiful also, and their straight column-like stems stand out in bold contrast to the rich luxuriance of many of the native trees. The shrub-tree of Killarney, the Arbutus of its native country and the winter strawberry of the strange **countries** into which it has been taken, is here, as everywhere where it is found, beautifully interesting. Its rich red berries shine through the waxy leaves with a brilliancy that commands admiring attention. Nor are the common hedgerow plants and flowers of the old country forgotten or neglected. The hawthorn is hard to cultivate, but it and its pinky-white and perfumed blossoms are by no means unknown. The sweetbriar is there too, and the woodbine; and in some instances they grow with a marvellous luxuriance. Jasmine and clematis there are **in** plenty, whilst orchids, distilling the most delicate perfumes, are **plentiful as** shells on the sea-beach. Tropical trees and fruits **grow, as a matter of** course, without trouble, and evidently enjoy **the climate to which** they have been transported. Among these latter **may be noted** trees useful as well as ornamental—whether all trees **and every plant does not** possess both of these characteristics may be fairly questioned—but the coffee, clove, pimento, cinnamon, and all the trees and shrubs that fill with perfume the shores **of** the Eastern seas, are here **cultivated with a** success that promises great things for their ultimate value to Queensland. That oranges and lemons, pine-apples and bananas, flourish in these well-kept gardens need hardly be told. Bananas, indeed, are far more plentiful in and around Brisbane than are potatoes in Ireland, or thistles in the "land of the mountain and the flood."

It would be unpardonable to take leave of the Brisbane Botanic Gardens without tendering a tribute of praise to its curator, Mr. Walter Hill. To this gentleman it is almost entirely due that the gardens have been brought to the excellence characteristic of them. He it was **who planted what** is now a grove of bamboo such as is rarely met with out of Queensland; scions of this cane will be all over the colony ere long. In addition to the labours that have made the Botanic Garden *the* lion of Brisbane, Mr. Hill has done right good service in searching for lands the best adapted for the cultivation of products not indigenous to Queensland. Thus he has journeyed up to the far north, and found land suitable for sugar growing on the banks of a score of rivers of greater or lesser extent. He has done more than this, for he has visited places before deemed inaccessible and discovered products before unknown. **Away** up on the height of Bellenden Kerr he found palm-trees grander **in their** proportions, perhaps, than any others in the world. On **one of his**

3 c

journeys he met with a so-called fig-tree, measuring—three feet from the ground—one hundred and fifty feet in circumference. This giant of the hitherto unknown forest was one hundred and eighty feet high at the point where it began to throw out its branches.

This would, perhaps, be as convenient a place as any in which to introduce a very brief description of some of the chief timber and other trees for which Queensland is famous. Many of them are not found near Brisbane, nor, indeed, in the districts surrounding, but a reference here will save divergence during a journey it will be necessary to take "up north," for the purpose of making the description of the country as perfect as possible. First of all, as well for its beauty as its usefulness, must be taken the Moreton Bay pine. Wherever seen it commands admiration; in outline it is perfect, and in colouring all that the artist could desire. To some extent it resembles the swamp oak of New South Wales, but it is far grander in its altitude and the beauty of its contour. It not unfrequently grows to a height of a hundred and fifty feet, and nearly every foot of the timber contained in the tree can be utilised for some valuable purpose. In this respect it equals the pine of Canada, and would indeed run closely that of the Baltic could it compete with it in European markets. Forests of Moreton Bay pine are confined to no particular locality of Southern Queensland. It grows on mountains and plains and alluvial flats alike, and everywhere it is "a thing of beauty" and value. The bunya bunya, another species of pine, is almost as useful, quite as beautiful, but not so widely distributed as is the Moreton Bay pine. From some specimens ships of the largest size could be fitted with masts in one piece; it bears a cone highly esteemed by the Blacks as food, whole tribes often travelling from two to three hundred miles, at the proper season, for the purpose of gathering and eating these cones. As in New South Wales, the red cedar abounds in Queensland, though in the Moreton Bay district it was for the most part destroyed many years ago. In 1875, one of the many digging parties who reached to the far north discovered a forest of red cedar extending several miles in length. This forest will doubtless be a source of wealth in future years, when the country towards Cape York is more settled upon. The boadab, or native fig-tree, although materially differing from the true boadab of Africa, is a useful and wonderful tree; its fruit is of exceeding value, and its wondrous growth, throwing down as it does its limbs to strike into the earth and so form other trees, makes it an object of exceeding interest wherever it is found. The

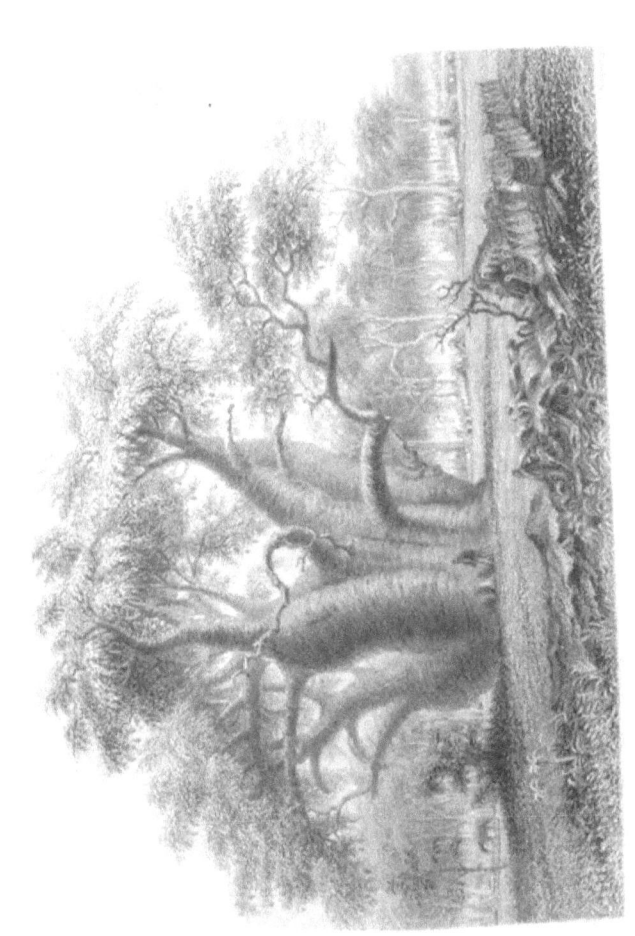

iron-bark and various gum-trees differ in no material particular from those of a similar description found in the neighbouring colonies and already described. The various perfumed trees of which mention has already been made are also found in Queensland, and applied to various industrial and ornamental purposes. As a rule the gum-trees of Northern Australia are richer in gum-producing qualities than those of the southern colonies. It is not a little curious that some of the most largely producing gum-trees grow on the poorest soils—on rocky and barren hill-sides, where the huge roots of the Eucalyptus are fain to run along the surface from sheer want of soil in which to bury themselves. The bark of these gum-trees, on being punctured, exudes masses of clear amber-coloured and sweet-smelling gum, that will surely be largely utilised by the manufacturers of the world some day or other. Some of the specimens exhibited in the Queensland annexe of the International Exhibition at South Kensington are of unusual beauty, and never fail to excite a pleasing and intelligent interest. Besides gums of worth, many of the trees and shrubs possess medicinal properties highly esteemed, and these also are becoming of merchantable value. The honey deposits of the trees should be by no means overlooked. Most of the Eucalypti bear flowers and blossoms, the nectaries of which are filled with the sweet fluid of which the native stingless bees of the country take full advantage. Their hives are built in the hollows of the trees themselves, and of this fact the natives were fully aware long before the white man competed with them for the possession of the soil. In the southern parts of the continent the black fellows adopted the plan of the American bee hunters, and fixed a few white filaments to the body of any bee they came across. By means of this they traced the scent-carrying flyer to its home and secured the contents of the hive. The aboriginal black of Northern Australia follows the line of flight taken by the bee by the keenness of his eyesight alone, and secures bee-bread and honey as the reward of his labour.

From this brief notice it can easily be imagined with what a brilliancy of colouring, beauty of outline, and perfumed air the people of Brisbane are surrounded. Nature has done much for Brisbane, but the presence of man has made it necessary that he should step in and bring art and science to bear upon his beautiful abiding-place. Of course the river has been improved and commodious wharves built, as has been seen. The houses and places of business are all most commendable, but the drainage of the town is somewhat defective. In the early months of 1875 preliminary steps were taken with a view to nullify this evil. It is to be hoped that, before the arrival in Brisbane of those who may be tempted by "AUSTRALIA ILLUSTRATED" to seek a home there, these things may be rectified, and the city made, what it easily might be, a model one.

It would be doing scant justice to Brisbane, or rather to Moreton Bay and the waters of the sea beyond, if reference to "the treasures of the deep" were not made. The finny and the shelly tribe abound in almost equal abundance one with the other. In the bay, and up and down the coast to the north and south of its entrance, fish swarm in countless shoals. To the south the dugong—the sea-cow it is not inaptly named—is found, and this fish, if fish it be, exists in great plenty. In size it is a monster, weighing from ten to twenty hundredweight, and not unfrequently measuring as many feet in length. Its flesh has always been highly esteemed by the natives, nor is this estimation less on the part of the white population. The dugong feeds on the delicate marine vegetation found in the shallow waters of the coast. Its flesh, when properly cured, is by no means bad succedaneum for a York ham, whilst the oil pressed from the fish would, if produced and prepared in sufficient quantities, form a formidable rival to the cod-liver oil with which children are not unfrequently overdosed in the old country. It is tasteless, and can be used with advantage in the preparation of cakes and pastry, and in such forms children—and grown-up people too, for that matter—gladly partake of it. In 1875 an experiment in tanning the skin of the dugong was made, and with the best possible results. From trials made of the first samples it was evident that, for driving-bands for machinery and for all other purposes for which heavy yet pliable leather is desirable, that the leather of the dugong was eminently superior to any hitherto in use. There is thus another valuable industry unexpectedly opened up. There will be a large industry springing up in connection with the dugong some day. Turtle are also plentiful in and around Moreton Bay, and large quantities are forwarded by steam to Sydney, Melbourne, and Adelaide. Other fish, for the most part similar to those referred to in connection with New South Wales, exist in great plenty on the Queensland coasts, and they only require to be looked after to prove a great source of wealth. All these things will be properly estimated by-and-by—indeed, to many of them attention has already been paid, and with gratifying results; and many of the now unconsidered sources of wealth will be adopted by home-seekers in addition to the ordinary and recognised industries of the colony.

CHAPTER XXI.

QUEENSLAND.—(*Concluded.*)

MEANS OF EDUCATION; ITS COST.—MANUFACTORIES.—GEOGRAPHICAL POSITION OF MORETON BAY; ITS FUTURE.—THE ISLANDS.—FROM BRISBANE TO GYMPIE.—THE PROSPECTORS FOR GOLD AND LAND.—A WORKED-FOR SUCCESS.—MARYBOROUGH.—THE LAKES.—GAYNDAH.—THE BURNETT.—BUNDERBERG—THE GREAT BARRIER REEF.—CORAL ISLANDS.—GLADSTONE.

BEFORE proceeding farther north, and whilst we are, as it were, in the heart of Queensland proper, it would seem convenient to introduce a few figures indicative of the progress of the colony, and its position in the year 1875.

At the time of the separation of the colony from New South Wales in **1859**, it contained a population numbering a little over 28,000 persons; in **1875 the population touched closely upon 170,000. In** 1860 its general **revenue amounted to £178,600. According to the most recent** returns, the **revenue exceeds that sum** by nearly a **million** pounds sterling, the actual amount being estimated at £1,170,000. The general expenditure had increased in a like ratio. The imports and exports tell the story of progressive prosperity even more significantly than the figures just quoted. In 1860 a few pounds over £742,000 included the whole purchasing powers of the Queenslanders from foreign countries; in 1875 the imports **were** worth £3,000,000. In the former year the exports were valued **at** £523,000, whilst in the latter year they reached nearly £4,000,000. **The** exports consisted of gold, copper, tin, wool, cotton, rice, sugar, hides, tallow, and preserved meats. Within the period referred to, the number of acres of land under cultivation had increased from about 3,300 to nearly 70,000 acres. Of this quantity, fully 15,000 acres are cultivated for sugar-making purposes. One or two other facts must close this somewhat dry, though very satisfactory, array of figures. In 1860 the deposits of money in the banks of the colony were considerably under £300,000; in 1875 such deposits amounted to nearly £3,000,000. To show that the mass of the people had participated in the prosperity indicated by these figures, it may be stated that in the latter-named year the deposits in savings banks amounted to nearly £605,000. The live stock of the colony at the same time was estimated at eight millions of sheep and a million and a half of cattle and horses. There were then some six hundred qualified teachers of the young engaged in the work of education. These were paid for their services by £45,000,

and the entire **contributions** towards education, including the erection of
school buildings, amounted to over £500,000. This **for a young colony
with a** population of about 170,000, must be looked upon **as a liberal**
contribution towards the development of the young people. **For the indoor**
employment of the industrial portion of the population there had been
established at the date named, four flour-mills, seventy mills for the crushing
of corn, and the manufacture of sugar; thirty steam-sawmills were engaged
in preparing the timber of the country for the purposes for which it was
designed; this, of course, quite apart from innumerable saw-pits **in active**
operation in every part of the colony. The preparation of cotton **for the**
English market gave employment to thirty guns, whilst in the preparation
of soap there were no less than "a baker's dozen" of manufactories engaged.
Meat-preserving had its interests attended to in half-a-dozen extensive
establishments, whilst distilleries, breweries, and other manufactures **of**
articles **in** general use, brought the number of industrial establishments up
to six hundred. That railways are by no means unknown in Queensland
has already been told. Nearly two millions and a half of pounds sterling
have been expended upon the construction of the iron way, and **the** expenditure is still proceeding. Before very many years have passed, Hobson's
Bay, Port Jackson, Moreton Bay, and Rockhampton, besides the numerous
towns and settlements lying between and beyond each, will have **a** line of
communication between them. South Australia is left out of the enumera-
tion because it will have its own line from gulf to gulf; and judging from
the enterprise manifested in carrying the telegraph line from the southern
to the northern shores of Australia, it is not impossible that South Australia
may carry away the honours in this particular.

Leaving the lake-like, because almost land-locked, waters of Moreton
Bay, and running up the coast towards the north, the most important
settlements of Queensland are to be met with, at an average distance of some
fifty miles from the Pacific. Before proceeding on the journey, however,
it will be desirable to present the more salient features of a harbour to
which there already belongs a history, and in connection with which it is a
safe prophecy to say great things may be expected in the future. Whether
disruption or confederation of the Australian colonies—and the former is
sure to precede the latter—takes place, it is certain that Moreton Bay
must, next to Port Jackson, hold the first position on the Pacific coast of
Australia. Other ports there are, farther north, possessing natural advantages equal to, if not surpassing, those of Moreton Bay, but the importance

of the country of which **it is the natural outlet can** never be taken away from it. **Moreton** Bay was the first **name given to what we** now call the colony of Queensland, and Moreton Bay will just as surely last as has Port Jackson and Sydney Harbour, notwithstanding **the** defection of Victoria, a portion of South Australia, and Queensland itself. Having thus achieved an importance that can never be totally eclipsed, it deserves a more lengthened notice than can be given to it in this place, but it must not be left wholly undescribed.

Moreton Bay then is, as may have already been gathered, not an indentation in the land merely. It is formed first of all by the mainland, and then by the islands running parallel thereto. These islands, three in number, are of very considerable extent. The southern, Stradbroke **Island**, is fully thirty miles from end to end: **at its lower, or** southern point, there is a narrow passage, **through which small craft** sometimes make their way into the bay. Moreton **Island comes next, and** measures some twenty miles in length, with an average width of three miles, or thereabouts. The northern, and smallest island of the three, is named Bribies Island, and between these two latter the chief entrance to Moreton Bay exists. The bay itself, sixty miles long, with an average width of twenty, contains a perfect archipelago of islands; the chief of these lie towards the southern extremity of the bay. For the most part, they are sufficiently picturesque in outline; excellent timber grows upon some of them, and **in** parts they are quite capable of being cultivated with profit. The same may be said of the landward side of the three principal islands; but on their Pacific shores they are simple sand-hills, but serving admirably as breakwaters against the long rollers of the ocean. Cleveland, a township on the shores of the bay, has a population of two hundred or so, and considerable quantities of sugar are grown in the neighbourhood.

Leaving Moreton Bay for the north, the country first passed over is, for the most part, of poor quality. Here and there are patches of good soil, and these have, of course, been utilised. After a small river, called the South River, has been crossed, better country is met with, and the land is admirably adapted for cultivation. The country assumes a picturesqueness of appearance wanting in the district immediately to the north of Brisbane. Wild fruits and flowers in infinite variety are to be found here in plenty; whilst the flowering shrubs are distinguished by an unusual beauty. The first point of much interest on the northern route is the township and gold-field of Gympie. The road from Brisbane to Gympie has been cut through a scrubby forest country that has tried the pluck and perseverance, sometimes to the "bitter end," of many a searcher for gold. The town is situated on the upper waters of the Mary River, and the country round about is, for the most part, diversified and pleasant to look upon. The immediate vicinity of the gold-diggings is bounded by a series of low-lying ranges and ridges, these again being encircled by hills of a similar character, but of greater altitude. The discovery of gold at Gympie was made about eight years after the rush to Rockhampton and Clermont, and was due to the experience then gained. The original discoverer was named Nash, and accordingly the first name given to the place was Nashville. Nash appears to have followed the profession of a prospector for gold in as nearly a systematic manner as possible. He was one of a class of men of which hundreds are to be found in every direction in the Australian colonies. They have a deep-seated belief in the undeveloped resources of the country, and devote their time to the development thereof. They are by no means confined to gold-seekers; they will go out prospecting for new and unsettled country, and then they are rightly entitled pioneers, or explorers. Others will travel week after week and month after month, in search of coal, or copper, or tin, or any other symbol of riches that most affects their fancy; these are called prospectors. Sometimes failure, sometimes success, rewards their efforts, and after much of striving, struggling, and suffering. Nash was one of the successful ones, and upon the hill-sides upon which he amused himself with picking nuggets of gold from out the interstices of the roots of the trees in 1867, there stands the prosperous and prospering town of Gympie. The alluvial lumps that first rewarded the exertions of Nash have pretty well disappeared now, but in their place the solid rocks have been opened up and forced to yield their treasure. Quartz-crushing machines abound in Gympie, and a large amount of capital has been invested in the various appliances of gold-mining. In common with nearly every Australian town, Gympie possesses its local newspaper, several banks, an excellent hospital, a school of art, a theatre, a masonic hall, and, as a matter of course, a court-house, in which justice is dispensed. Places of worship and public-houses are in about equal proportion, and they are all well patronised. A good many farms are to be found in the neighbourhood, and the farmers, or settlers, as they are usually called, are a prosperous race; their products being chiefly maize, fruits, and vegetables—these, of course, are always in demand.

Before descending towards the coast—and this rule of proceeding will have to be adopted on many occasions during the description of the settled portions of Queensland—it may be noted that towards the north and west several other gold-fields exist. Copper has been found and profitably worked on the banks of the Burnett, the most considerable river north of the Mary, and due north of Gympie the coal measures of the colony become distinctly developed. Nearly the whole of this country is covered with open forest and scrub, interspersed here and there with agricultural land of an excellent character. Beyond the coal country, the main or dividing range of mountains runs in far towards the west, and beyond these, the vast plains of the interior extend right across Queensland, and into the northern territory of South Australia.

Running down the River Mary, and within sixty miles of the mouth thereof, the town of Maryborough is met with. This is the shipping port and principal town of the Wide Bay and Burnett districts, and is one of the most important sugar and cotton-growing localities of Queensland. The town and district contains fully ten thousand persons, and promises to grow in importance and extent for many years to come. It has two capitally conducted newspapers, the *Maryborough Chronicle* and the *Wide Bay and Burnett News*. Half-a-dozen banks have branches or agencies in the town, which enjoys the privilege also of an excellently selected public library. Places of worship are sufficiently plentiful, and are all of them well supported. The forests round about abound with timber of a valuable quality, and the scenery has all the charms of a semi-tropical country. The sugar-cane grows plentifully in all the rich flats bounding the river, and its cultivation is one of the chief industries of the district. Cotton-growing is also a valuable industry hereabouts, and the quality of the fibre is said to be unexceptionable. Some of the samples forwarded to England have been highly esteemed by those best able to judge, whilst the crops of maize may be pronounced fairly marvellous. Side by side with the ordinary productions of an English market-garden may be found pine-apples, bananas, guavas, and all the most delicious fruits of the best fruit-producing countries of the world. The climate is all that could be desired. There are few extreme changes of temperature; hot winds are hardly known; women and children flourish and enjoy robust health, and the average rainfall is sufficient for all the purposes of irrigation. The river and bay abound with delicious fish; minerals are plentiful, and only await enterprise and capital to develop their value.

Wide Bay lies to the south and east of Maryborough, and between

SANDY CAPE.

Port Curtis or Keppel Bay on the other. To this port comes the copper from Mount Perry, and the produce of a considerable distance round about; sugar is a favourite crop with the farmers; who, however, by no means fail to bestow the requisite attention to the cultivation of cereals and fruits. Coal exists in the neighbourhood, and will doubtless be profitably worked at no distant day.

Before taking an absolute departure from Harvey Bay it is desirable that one of the chief physical features of this part of the world should be referred to. In doing so, we shall be taken far beyond the point with which this portion of AUSTRALIA ILLUSTRATED is concerned, but we shall thereby be saved the perplexity of referring to the subject on divers occasions. Great Sandy Island has already been spoken of. It is a long sandy ridge almost touching at its southern point, in Wide Bay, the mainland of Australia. From the bay named, it runs almost parallel with the coast, until, where Harvey Bay proper commences, it takes an easterly course and terminates nearly opposite, though at a considerable distance from, an inconsiderable stream called the Kolan River. The northern extremity of Great Sandy Island is, appropriately enough, named Sandy Cape. The name Sandy describes with sufficient accuracy cape and island. North of this cape, however, a few features in the land or sea-scape is revealed. Here commences the great barrier reef of Australia. This is unexceptionably the most wonderful coral formation in the world. It extends from Sandy Cape to the Gulf of Carpentaria, and is probably continued along the south, eastern, and northern shores of New Guinea. This would give it a course from south to north of fully twelve hundred miles. The rocks and islands of which it is composed vary in size, but the mean breadth of the reef may be taken at about thirty miles. Stretching away into the Pacific there are doubtless innumerable and hitherto-unnoted islands forming portions of the one grand system built up through countless ages by the tiny coral insect whose persistent labours go so far to form a world. These latter islands stretching as they do to New Caledonia on the east, and New Guinea on the west, the reef may safely be put down as extending fully six hundred miles from west to east. It would be impossible to over-estimate the beauty of some of these islands; they are perfect in outline and clothed with a delicious verdure. Their mimic mountains and valleys, their tiny streams, umbrageous shrubs and pleasant plains present scenes of ever-varying beauty to the voyager who cruises among them. Sometimes the more prominent features of their coasts assume quaint fantastic shapes; the valleys appear as though peopled with **fauns and** dryads, tiny **waterfalls** leap from ledge **to ledge** of miniature precipices, and, mingling their waters with the quiet **streams of** the coral land, look like rivers upon whose bosom the unknown **life of the** island could be borne into the vast ocean **that washes two** continents. Some day this vast archipelago will be perhaps as famous as the "isles of Greece," and Australian poets sing their praises with a warmth of language worthy of their beauty.

These coral reefs have their dark sides, however. Amid some of them it is dangerous to sail in daylight, for beneath the waves that ripple so gently, or lash with fury against the shores of the seen, lie the terrible dangers of the unseen—jagged peaks and rocks are there, and woe to the ship whose keel touches them. It was on such a rock the *Gothenburg* met her fate, and how many a ship that has "sent for answer back" has taken its living freight to death in the same southern waters will never be known. Of late years a good many of the main features of the reef have been laid down and, **under** ordinary circumstances, the navigation of the waters of the various **straits** and passages is by no means a work of very great difficulty. For hardy small craft, it **would** not be easy to find more pleasant cruising ground. Some day it will be one of the show-places of the world, to which yachters will resort. Every port in Australia has its fleet of yachts, now-a-days. The coasts of California are admirably adapted for yachting. **The** islands lying between that mainland and the east coast of Australia would make admirable calling-places, and sailing matches between San Francisco and the ports of Queensland need by no means be numbered among the most improbable things of the future; they would furnish contests worthy of men belonging to the British race.

Returning to the mainland, the next point of interest met with is Port Curtis, with the town of Gladstone on the shores thereof. At one time it appeared certain that Gladstone would be the chief town of this part of Queensland. The hope thus conveyed has not been realised, for Rockhampton on the Fitzroy has just as decidedly taken the position that Gladstone was intended to occupy, as Melbourne has of that of Geelong, or that Mr. Disraeli has of the statesman after whom Gladstone was called. **The** port of Gladstone—a very excellent one, by-the-bye—is formed by an irregularly formed detached piece of land called Facing Island, and the mainland. The surroundings of the port are very beautiful, and seemingly well adapted for the position of an important centre of commerce and population. It is perfectly land-locked and capable of sheltering a large fleet of large ships.

Years ago it was described as "a noble port capable of floating all the *Great Easterns* in the world." Having in view that there is only one *Great Eastern*, this may not seem very high praise, but the describer was doubtless speaking in figurative language. The same writer describes Port Curtis as being one of the most magnificent in the South Seas, happily situated, not only geographically, but because of the salubrity of its climate and gentleness of temperature—it enjoys a cool sea-breeze all the year round, and experiences no great extremes of heat or cold. Notwithstanding this opinion there pertains to it varied peculiarities, and the seasons are somewhat precarious. Although the country round about is, in common with most of Australia, subject to heavy floods, they do little permanent damage. Within twenty-four hours of the heaviest rains the floods subside, leaving behind them germs of fertility and fruitfulness, that for some time repay the temporary inconvenience they may have caused. In 1855, three years, it will be remembered, before the great gold rush that brought the first actual importance to Queensland, a government authority reported that, in his opinion, Gladstone would be one of the most important cities of the eastern seaboard of Australia. This prophecy has not yet been realised, but the logic of events may still make it true. When the news of the discovery of gold at Canoona reached the southern colonies, Port Curtis was the destination of every ship laid on for the new gold-field. The old reports of the harbour were remembered, and the traffic was attracted thither in consequence. Before many ships had sailed, however, rumours of another and a better port, that of Keppel Bay, were received, and the traffic was at once directed to the northern end of the Sandy spit. Gladstone, after a thoroughly governmental fashion, had been quietly content to view the good fortune that had so unexpectedly fallen in its way, and the affair was received as a distinct reward of merit and superiority. This was not to last long, however, and within a week the town sank back into its former position of insignificance, and Rockhampton progressed in proportion. Captain O'Connell, the then government resident, had to acknowledge the truth of the saying that "hope is not prophecy," and exchange the tranquil official delights of Gladstone for the somewhat turbulent racket of Rockhampton. The state of things thus indicated has never been reversed, and Gladstone continues to this day a pleasant, but by no means lively town. Being Australian, its streets are of course well laid out; its public and private buildings are perhaps better than many of those of its more pretentious and go-ahead rival, but it remains a quiet country-place, instead of the "impor-

or about the parallel of 25° south, "nature had set up landmarks not to be disputed." When the division of Northern from Southern Queensland comes about, the point arrived at will doubtless be not far off the starting line for each colony, and on this account it is convenient to adopt the plan proposed. The division thus indicated will not be simply a geographical one, for there are special features, social, industrial, and political, characteristics of the north of Queensland, that are sure some day to separate it from the south. The distance of the northern portions of the colony from the seat of government is certain to be an operative influence in the matter; whilst north of the tropical line it is that the question of coolie labour in Australia will have to be settled. The experiment is going on, and will have to be referred to when the new northern settled country comes to be described.

First in point of distance and of importance in **the** portion of the description now entered upon, comes Rockhampton, and its port Keppel Bay. This latter is situated as nearly as possible on the tropical line of Capricorn. The story of the first settlement on the banks of the Fitzroy has already been told in these pages. The bay, although not so well sheltered as Port Curtis or Moreton Bay, is a sufficiently safe and commodious one. On entering the river, one of the first peculiarities that strikes the visitor is the low-lying banks, bounded alternately on either **side** by stretches of melancholy-looking mangrove and open forest land. Wherever the mangrove abounds the banks are low and intersected with numerous creeks. The shores are composed of rich black soil, having all the characteristics of a tropical swampy country. Wherever the forest lands appear the banks are higher, and although of no very great elevation, **present a** sheer fall from the table-lands to the waters of the river. **One other** peculiarity may be noted: the sand-banks with which the river is every here and there intersected appear to follow, by a natural law, the characteristics of the banks themselves—where the mangrove grows the bed of the river has silted up, and under the high walls the water is deep; and when the indications thus offered are followed the navigation is safe. This was manifested on many occasions when the first rush to Canoona took place by the stranding of many of the craft that attempted the passage up the river upon the low-lying shores with which the mangrove was bounded. In times of flood, vessels, tempted by the depth of water, ventured too close into the low river side and were carried ashore. It was no uncommon circumstance then to see craft lying high and dry—after the subsidence of the tide, of course—among the tree-like scrub on the northern banks of the river. As the upper reaches of the stream were reached these casualties decreased, until, approaching the site of the present town of Rockhampton, they disappeared altogether. Notwithstanding these difficulties, the Fitzroy struck the new-comer as being a river of a highly important character. It was impossible to sail upon its then almost unknown waters without being impressed with the conviction that it formed the natural drainage channel of an immense country. At the mouth of the river, and for a good many miles above it, the tributary streams crept into it as it were with a slow, sluggish motion. Many were the tales of disaster told of those who had ventured to land upon the low-lying flats with which the stream was bounded. As the river was followed, however, these disagreeable and dangerous phases were lost, and as Rockhampton was approached, although the northern banks were still low and ominous-looking, the river assumed more perfect proportions, and presented a pleasing contrast to the non-tidal streams with which most of the adventurers from the other colonies were best acquainted.

Rockhampton itself, although not highly elevated, is by no means unfavourably positioned. The banks of the river are sufficiently well-defined and abrupt to leave the water way by the side of the town clear. South of the town the country is flat and here and there broken by lakes and lagunes that add an element of beauty and usefulness not to be despised in so warm a country. The margins of these lagunes and in many places the banks of the river are often masses of flowers. Water-flags and lilies of unusual beauty abound, and when, during the warm summer nights, their bright purple bells are filled by the ever-flitting fire-flies, with their perpetually scintillating lights, the scene may, with considerable appropriateness, be described as fairy-like. Most of the land is a rich dark loam, and the natural grasses of the district contain nutritive qualities of unusual excellence. Just above Rockhampton a ledge of rocks runs across the river, forming what are called the Falls or Rapids, and beyond these falls the country rapidly opens and becomes still more interesting and diversified in its features. The Fitzroy continues to be a fine broad stream with depth sufficient to float vessels of considerable size; the banks of the river become bolder and more defined, whilst the scrub country almost disappears and an open forest country is on every side. The mountains stand out in the distance, some of their sides glittering with the white marble of which they are composed. Wherever tributary creeks or water-courses join the river, the banks are for the most part low-lying, and on these flats the richest possible land is met with. They

ALLIGATORS.   205

are, of course, liable to inundation; but **the floods** enrich the already **luxuriant soil to** an extent that far more **than** repays the farmer for the **damage they do. On these flats** or swamps the trees grow to an enormous size, and are festooned **in** every direction by wild vines and creepers, many of the latter bearing flowers of exceeding richness of colouring and gracefulness of form. Nor is the vegetation the only tropical product of the place: here the alligator is said to find a home, though, to his credit be it said, he rarely puts in an appearance—in **truth, the** alligator is somewhat of a mythical personage on the banks of the rivers of Queensland. Every settler has his own legend to tell of an alligator he has either seen or shot, but there is seldom any evidence of the fact; the stories serve **to** beguile the travellers into a belief of the dangers he may possibly meet with, and that is **about** the only purpose the alligators of the Fitzroy fulfil. They **are not** desirable acquaintances, and the smallness of their number is not complained of.

Some of the characteristics of the Fitzroy have been excellently described in various letters to the Australian newspapers. One such description says—"The river widens out into a magnificent sheet of water, overhung on each side **with** immense tea-trees which project far into the waters below. These trees are very different from the stunted small-leaved specimens found farther south. The leaves are long, straight, and pendant; the leaf-bearing twigs drooping down from the boughs pretty much after the same fashion as those of the weeping-willow, which thus far the tea-tree of the Fitzroy **much** resembles. On the extremity of many of the twigs, and generally five or six feet above the water, the tailor bird builds its nest: these are very beautiful specimens of bird-architecture. They are formed by intertwining leaves with small twigs, pieces of moss and wool, and soft pieces of bark. The entrance to the nest is at the top and is protected by a long eave, thus securing the young birds from the weather, from snakes, iguanas, and other enemies from which the parent birds know it **to be** necessary to protect their young. In addition to this," the writer proceeds, "I observed, in several places where the bank of the river was bare and precipitous, and where portions of it had been washed out or fallen, thus forming a hollow, that large numbers of a small kind of marten had congregated together. They were busily engaged constructing nests of mud, which were ranged in long close lines on the roof of the hollow. The little creatures were all occupied at their work—some at the water's edge working up and tempering the clay; others clinging to **the** half-formed nests, beating in with their wings the clay already prepared by their mortar-mixing fellows. At this part of the river in South Australia I see for the first time a very beautiful tree, which we know well under planting as he mounted the stream. It had a large bright leaf, very much resembling that of the top in shape, but darker in colour. The branches spread out almost at right angles from the trunks, but instead of forming a series of rings, as in the case of the fir, they were indented, getting shorter as they reached the top. Through such scenery he travelled for nine miles, his boatmen pulling against a strong down current. On landing on a small island, he discovered a store of "stones and pebbles that" (said he) "gladdened the heart of a geologist." Further on, he says: "We once more embarked, the business of pulling the boat against the stream becoming a very serious one, more especially as the river, near the corner in such places running so swiftly as to give the two rapid as much as they **could** **to** make head against it. At the end of a few safety points the first rapids occur, the river being narrowed to one-third of its ordinary width. A long pull and a strong pull was necessary to get over the difficulty, and then we had before us, for a distance of nine or ten miles the same broad sheet of water, the same open banks, and the same luxuriant vegetation that had characterised the former part of the journey. There would have been a sameness in the unvaried richness of the shores on either side, were it not that at intervals creeks made their way in through the high banks, breaking them up sometimes into small islets, sometimes into long jutting peninsulas, and always forming minor deltas, upon which vegetation was wild and profuse. Here and there deep bays occurred, their placid waters, which the current did not reach, having a surface smooth and polished as a sheet of glass."

Whilst the Fitzroy itself flows through not only a beautiful country, but one rich in its soils, timbers, and minerals, north-west of its head waters there lies a district of considerable importance. At this point the coal measures of Queensland would be pierced at their widest part. Beyond this coal country, or rather just where a "fault" in the formation seems to occur, one of the most important copper deposits of the colony is situated. The celebrated Peakdown mine, with its district town Clermont, is to be found here. Auriferous ground is not wanting either, and altogether a great future may be pretty safely predicted for this part of the country.

To return to the Fitzroy, however; and it being a typical river of

Northern Australia, it is, apart from the interest that pertains to it by itself, worthy of extended notice here, because what is said of it now will serve in some degree as a description of many of the river courses met with farther north. A party of diggers who had been prospecting for gold on the Fitzroy and its higher tributaries decided on returning to Rockhampton, and their experiences on the journey will give as vivid an idea of the river for the greater portion of its course as could possibly be obtained. The means of conveyance was, of course, the first consideration, and for this purpose the bottle-tree offered itself in abundance. This tree the adventurers described, in homely but perfectly understandable language, as being in shape like a lemonade-bottle, small at **the bottom,** bulging out as it rose towards **the centre, and gradually contracting until** it ran up like the neck of a **bottle—hence, of course, its name.** The bark is very hard, **with** a rough exterior resembling **the** outer covering of a tree known in these regions as the mountain-oak. When the outer **covering** is removed, the inner bark is found to be harder than the hardest **heart of oak,** requiring an exceedingly well-tempered axe wielded by a **skilful arm to penetrate it.** Once through this defence, however, the work **of manipulating the timber is easy.** The interior of the tree is soft **as the stalk of a cabbage, and the natives,** when short of better **food, often eat it raw. It is** rich **and** unctuous, and not much unlike a cocoa-**nut.** The process of boiling improves its quality; it then becomes **a** jelly little inferior to the best arrowroot, the which it somewhat resembles in flavour. The leafy top that crowns the stalk, for it can hardly be called a trunk, is erect and spreads considerably, assuming somewhat the character of the fern-tree; the leaves, however, being more like those of the oak. The stems rise to a height of from twenty to twenty-five **feet, and when** hollowed they, as may be readily understood from the description given of the inner bark, form capital canoes. In such a **boat,** the party of prospectors determined to make their journey of over **two** hundred miles to Rockhampton. The length of the boat, or "dug-out," as they called it, was sixteen feet; it was nearly four feet wide at its widest part, and had a depth of a foot and a half. They left the bottom precisely as nature had formed it, and luckily so, for on the voyage they discovered that the natural form of the tree was the best possible for the work they had undertaken. She ran over logs, snags, and sawyers in perfect safety, and was adapted for resisting any ordinary obstruction with which she might be brought into collision.

This rude boat was launched on the waters of the Dawson, the tributary of the Fitzroy, from which the star was made—just as the last sun of December was making itself felt. For an account of the journey took the words of the journeyers may with perfect propriety be adopted. "On the 5th of December," they say, "we launched our dug-out on the waters of the Dawson, and occupied ourselves for the remainder of the day in chopping our paddles for use when we might require them. We may mention here that the mountains on the Dawson, all throughout where we have been, are very high and heavy, seeming to ascend one over the other, tier above tier, that they are composed of a compact sandstone, cropping up here and there through the shallow soil with which they are covered. The valleys are exceedingly rich. The grass grows shoulder-high, and a man walking through it can hardly be distinguished a dozen feet away. The soil is good, and apparently well adapted for cultivation. Before starting on our journey we, as sensible men would, took stock, and found our provisions to consist of forty pounds of flour, a fore-quarter of mutton, eight pounds of sugar, and a pound of tea." The reader should bear in mind that thus provisioned, these four Australian diggers started on a journey of an unknown distance, and down a river upon the higher waters of which a white man had never heretofore been seen.

The narrative proceeds: "On the 5th December, having loaded old dug-out, we shoved him boldly into the current, which was running at the rate of seven knots an hour. This was the rate according to Mr. Mackenzie, who came to see us start, and who accompanied us some distance on the way. We imagine we must have gone about the same rate wherever rapids occurred; but there were places where the stream widened out and became deeper, and where the current had consequently less effect; sometimes, indeed, we had to pull in order to hasten our progress. The rapid referred to extended for a distance of about eight miles, rather a long stretch for a fall of the kind. In this way we proceeded, sometimes pulling hard, at others whirled off by the current, until at six in the evening we reached the junction of the waters of the Dawson and Mackenzie, where the united waters became the river Fitzroy.

"This junction is supposed to be, as the crow flies, about thirty-eight miles nearly due north from Rio station. The confluence of the streams forms a very beautiful sheet of water about a quarter of a mile in width and extended away as far as the eye could reach, until lost in the magnificent trees that border it. We have reason to believe that we were the first

white men that ever floated boat or canoe over the confluence of the two rivers. At seven in the evening we went ashore and camped on the banks of the Fitzroy, about six miles below the junction. On the 6th, at daylight, we again manned our canoe and travelled down the river—no pleasant road—over snags, and logs, and rocks, and downfalls, and along rapids. During this day we met with more than the usual number of bars across the river. These were composed of a blue rock, much harder than the ordinary slaty bars of auriferous rivers, and also closer in the grain and much smoother than the trap rock we have to go through in many deep sinkings in our search for gold. These places struck us as being likely spots for gold, but our provisions were low and we had to push on in spite of everything. The rapids here—and, in fact, all up the river —are marked by a thick tea-tree scrub that grows right across and in the bed of the river, so closely that at times the passage through is hardly perceptible. At 7 P.M. we camped for the night on the banks of the river, a sheet of calico our only covering; the uncertainty of our position causing us to husband our provisions by partaking only of a light supper. On the 7th we passed through a very heavy range of mountains, through which the river had cut itself a sinuous course, flowing through the wildest and most magnificent scenery. On the next day, December 8, we came early in the day to a white mountain, which we at first took to be a quartz hill. We therefore landed and examined it, and on closer inspection found it to consist of white marble, that was everywhere broken and scattered on the surface, until the hill looked as though it was covered with snow. The marble was exceedingly white and delicate, without veins of any kind through it, so far as we could see from the surface indications. We had no time to make further examination, for our provisions were all but gone and we had to hurry on to some quarter where a further supply was obtainable. We, however, ascended to the top of the hill, and there, stretching away to the westward, could see mountains to a distance of forty miles, lifting up their heads into the clouds, and clad in robes as white as those worn by the Alps in winter time. We imagined these hills to be about one hundred and forty miles from Rockhampton, at which place we arrived on the 12th, having during the two previous days passed many rapids and falls, and having fortunately fallen in with a party by whom we were generously supplied with provisions sufficient to carry us to the end of our journey. On the 11th, we were about thirty miles from Canoona." The adventurers wind up their narrative by saying, "Such is the simple unvarnished tale of an expedition that gave us an insight into the interior of a country little known, and made us acquainted with a means of conveyance of which few had hitherto dreamt. Our party on starting had been informed that the blacks were very numerous on the upper Dawson and the upper Fitzroy, but not one was seen, although the numerous fires burning on the banks, and many recent traces of their presence, showed that they had only just cleared out before the white invader of their domain.

Since the journey referred to was taken a change has been wrought, and on the banks of the Fitzroy and its tributaries. Some of the most valuable cattle stations in the world have been formed and worked on the lands through which the travellers passed. Other settlements of a still more valuable and interesting character have taken place. Of course, wherever gold and copper has been found—and such discoveries have been made in every direction, and at comparatively short distances apart—populations varying in number, and institutions varying in kind and character, have been permanently established. The repeated discovery of other ores has also the effect of promoting the migration and subsequent settlement of large bodies of people. Iron, lead, bismuth, antimony, mercury, and manganese ores have all been found, and although the development of the various mines, when compared with gold, is slow, still the work goes on, and future and permanent prosperity is sure to be the result. While speaking of metals it may be as well to say that gems and precious stones are met with in widely different districts of Queensland—diamonds and opals, the latter in considerable quantities; whilst sapphires, turquoises, and garnets are found in most of the auriferous drifts of the colony.

The agricultural and pastoral settlement is, after all, the most valuable and interesting. The latter has resulted in the shipment of immense quantities of wool to England; while the former has developed sugar, and cotton, and corn to an extent the earlier settlers had no conception of. To the pastoral pursuits must also be credited the shipments of preserved meats to England, that, thanks to the exertions of the celebrated Tallerman and others, have done so much towards feeding the people of England, and keeping the price of animal food within something like reasonable limits.

To return to Rockhampton. The beginnings of the town have already been described. According to the most recent authority—the admirably compiled handbook of Messrs. Gordon and Gotch for 1876—" Rockhampton may be considered the **capital of Northern** Queensland." "It is," **says** the authority referred to, "an **important town,** under municipal government, on the Fitzroy **River,** 45 **miles from its** mouth, and about 420 miles north-west of Brisbane. **It is in the county** of Livingstone, and owes its rise **to** the great Port Curtis rush. It is the port of shipment for a large extent **of** back country, and also for some of the produce of the Peak Downs copper and gold mines. Late returns enumerate the exports as follows:—Wool, 15,000 bales; gold, 10,000 ounces; copper, about 1,000 tons; besides hides, tallow, preserved meats, &c. It is also the starting-point of the Great Northern Railway, which at present reaches to Rocky Creek, **about** 44½ miles distant. The extension to the Mackenzie River, 125 miles from **Rockhampton, and** 99 from Peak Downs, is being vigorously carried on by **means of a loan of £480,000, sanctioned** by parliament two years since. **The number of the inhabitants is 5,500,** and, with the vicinity, 6,500. The **streets are wide and well planned, the principal** thoroughfare being East Street, ornamented with numerous **stone and other** buildings. Among the latter are the places of worship, Episcopalian, Roman Catholic, Presbyterian, **two** Wesleyan churches, one Baptist, one Primitive, and one Lutheran; the hospital, salubriously situated, and accommodating 40 patients; a school of arts, possessing a library of nearly 3,000 volumes; the supreme court buildings and government offices, gaol, police office, and barracks, Town Hall, Masonic Hall, Oddfellows' Hall, and an orphanage. The Union, Australian, Joint-Stock, Queensland, and National Australian banks have branches in the town; and the United, Australian General, London and Liverpool, and Globe insurance companies are all represented by agencies. A useful mercantile institution is the chamber of commerce recently established, and consisting of 40 members. There are 76 miles of roads and streets in the municipality, and about 1,100 dwellings, the rateable value of the property being nearly £661,000. The works for supplying the town with gas are completed, and the streets are now lighted up. The town is well supplied with water brought from extensive lagunes some two miles distant, and pumped by steam power into an artificial reservoir at the summit of an intervening range 150 feet in height. The gold-fields in the vicinity of Rockhampton give employment to 1,264 miners, about 220 **of** them being Chinese. There are 10 quartz-crushing machines, **having an** aggregate of 114 horse-power, the total mining plant being valued **at** £20,000. Minerals are widely diffused, gold, silver, and copper **deposits** being **now** worked within a radius of 40 miles **from the** town. **About**

4 miles [...] of the Central Queensland [Meat-Preserving Company, which employs] upwards of 100 hands. Other [...] a tannery, two soap factories, and two or three [...]. The town is surrounded with land [...] for [grazing] purposes. The [Fitzroy and Thompson rivers] run [...] is being rapidly [...] and [...]

CHAPTER XXIII.

NORTHERN AUSTRALIA.

MACKAY — BOWEN — TOWNSVILLE — THE PEARL-FISHERIES — CARDWELL — THE PALMER RIVER GOLDFIELDS — COOKTOWN — CAPE YORK — NORMANTON — THE QUEENSLAND TELEGRAPH LINE — OVERLAND TO SOUTH AUSTRALIAN BORDER — PORT DARWIN — THE SOUTH AUSTRALIAN TELEGRAPH — THE FAR WEST.

The space available in this work will render it necessary that the descriptions of the settlements and scenery of the north-east coast, and the vast inland districts they bound, should be somewhat of the briefest. Indeed, in writing of Australia generally, this same want would be felt; but in no part of the continent more than in the district just entered upon. The whole country is full of interest. Here it was that Leichardt pursued his first journeys, and from that day to this it has been the favourite hunting ground of the pioneer and explorer. These have been unceasing in their efforts, and consequently the making of history is a very rapid process. This fact will be gathered very intelligently and significantly from the slight descriptions given of the various points on the journey. Nearly the whole district is of unusual richness—no finer harbours, richer pasture-lands, better breeding grounds, or more prosperous industries of various kinds exist in the world. Its forests are far-stretching and filled with timber, nearly always of a valuable kind.

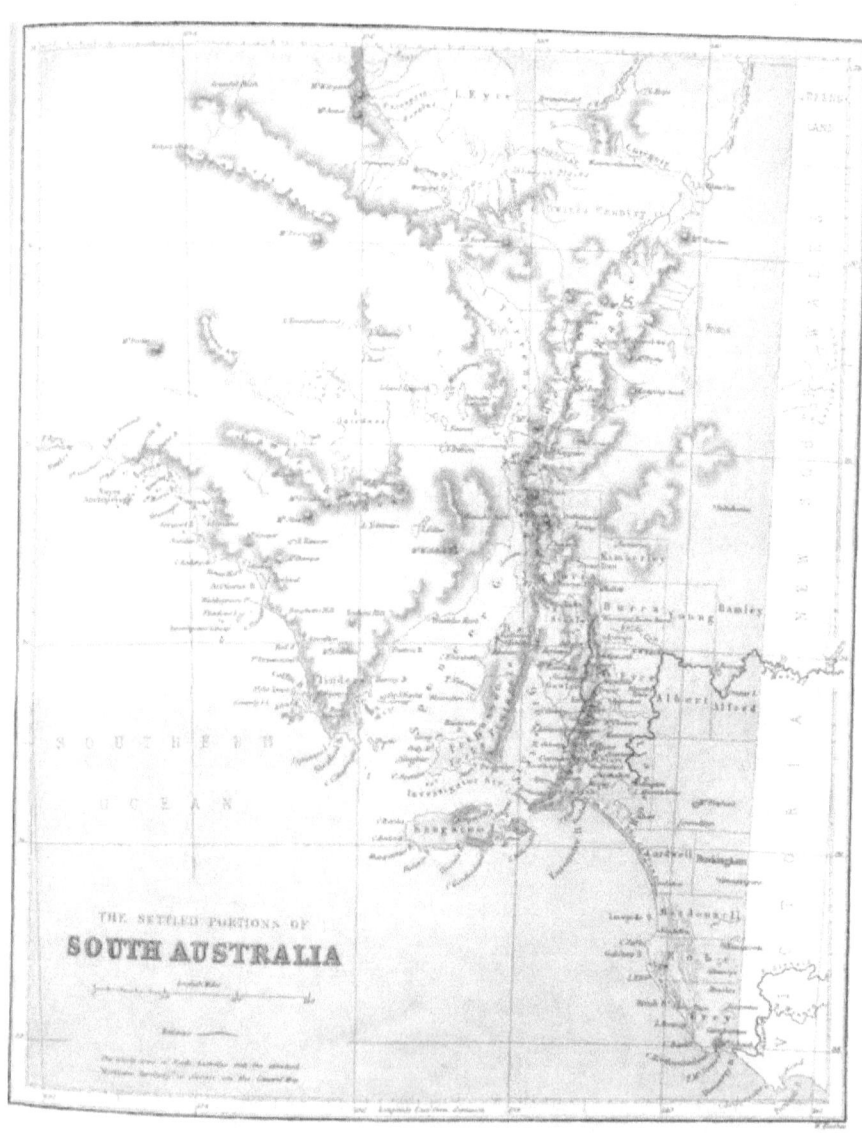

SUGAR-GROWING. 213

Its rivers and bays abound in fish, and in some places on the coast pearls are **plentiful** "**as** leaves in Vallombrosa." The mountains are striking in their **outlines, and by no** means insignificant in altitude. The congregations of **men to be met with are** of a varied character, and among them is being **worked out several** problems in social **and** political economy of no mean importance.

Mackay is the next really important place met with after leaving Rockhampton, although, according to seniority, it should give place to the town of Bowen, situate farther north. Mackay is the great centre of the sugar-growing industry of Queensland. In 1875 nearly half of the whole sugar produce of Queensland came from around Mackay and the banks of the river whose name it bears. For so young a place, it is not a small matter that in the year just named six thousand tons of sugar were grown and made in the district. In connection with this crop of sugar the employment of Polynesian labour naturally crops up, and in connection with that labour one of the social problems of Queensland, already referred to, is involved. Its discussion would be out of place here, but it may be stated that under ordinarily wise and ordinarily well administered regulations, there appears no reason **why the labourers** of the South Seas should not be profitably and pleasantly **employed in** this and other districts of the "Queen of Colonies." Whilst the **white man, the Briton** especially, is quite capable of pursuing all ordinary **out-door** employments and amusements in Northern Australia, it appears pretty certain that the cultivation of sugar and cotton and rice is beyond him, and, just where he is wanted, the Coolie and the South-Sea Islander step in, and upon their shoulders, under proper supervision, must devolve the development of, at any rate, the rich low-lying lands of Northern Australia. Nor will this fashion of the apportionment of labour be left entirely in the hands of Europeans. In connection with a part of the country still farther north than the Mackay, and to which further reference will have to be made, the Chinaman has made himself a power in the land, and whatever he may be in his own country, the Chinaman is by no means a non-progressive creature in Australia. The course he runs may appear a slow one, but it is generally sure. On the gold **fields a** Chinaman will make a living where a white man **would** starve: then again, as to climate and the thousand and one inconveniences of which Englishmen complain, the Chinaman seems positively to enjoy them—the heat that makes thin the blood and dissolves the brain of the white man is to him a genial and welcome warmth; mosquitoes he treats with quiet contempt, whilst hot winds and dust storms simply remind one of the Flowery Land, to return to which one day is the great and absorbing desire of his life, and he is more than content. To these men it will remain, in a very great measure, to solve the problem of **the utilisation of the** natural riches of Northern Australia.

The town of Mackay may be very briefly described. It is an out of the way sort of **place, but** prosperous notwithstanding. There are nearly a thousand people resident in **the** town, those in the outlying districts bringing the number up to five thousand. In addition to sugar, coffee and tobacco thrive. Wherever there is sugar-cane follows as a natural consequence, and four distilleries of raw spirit may be found at work in the town of Mackay. It is not a good sheep country, but horses and cattle flourish, and the richness of the land and salubrity of the climate is testified **to** by the luxuriant growth of indigenous and introduced plants.

Running the coast up from Mackay to Bowen, the islands already referred **to** are met with plentifully; indeed, the whole country is of a diversified and pleasant character. Threading through these islands, after leaving Repulse Bay, Port Denison is reached. In common with several other harbours already referred to, Port Denison claims to be the "first harbour in Queensland." Whether this be so or no, it is certain that it forms the outlet for one of the richest portions of the north-eastern districts of the continent; nature has adapted it most admirably to this purpose. At this point the coast range makes a considerable bend towards the west, and thus a large area of coast-land is left to be taken advantage of by the industry and perseverance of man. For fully five hundred miles west of Port Denison there is not a single mountain of importance to be met with; gentle rises there are in plenty, and here and there ranges of altitude sufficiently commanding to give a picturesque aspect to the country—these notwithstanding, there is a vast territory ready for the plough. In many directions not even a stump or a **rock** interposes between the desire of the settler to cultivate the land and the realisation of his wish. The soil is rich beyond all that has been told of the rolling prairies of the north-west of Canada and the corn-lands of the United States. On the banks of the Bowen river, for scores and scores of miles, there are alluvial flats that may be cropped **with** the most exhausting products for years and years to come, without the natural richness of the soil being exhausted. West of the low dividing range similar characteristics pertain to the country. Here, indeed, the available plain-land may, with all propriety, be described as boundless. The climate on these comparatively elevated champaign countries possesses all the

THE BURDEKIN.

attributes of pleasantness that man need desire; and on these "Darling Downs of the North," as they have been not unaptly described, there is verge and scope enough for all the workers that Great Britain could spare for any defined decade. Through this country flows a river that may be fairly called the "father of waters," for at short intervals it parts with branches of its noble self that will prove sources of riches to the dwellers on their banks so long as the great south land endures. The river Burdekin traverses for hundreds of miles a very Garden of Eden. No matter whether it flows with slow and sluggish stream through rich flats, or glides swiftly by the few projections that at rare intervals intrude upon its course, it carries the germs of infinite richness along with it. Nor, when the lands become less fertile, does the natural value of the surroundings of the river decrease. Gold abounds in plenty on the banks of the tributaries of the Burdekin, and other valuable minerals and gems are to be found for the looking for. Nor is it to the west alone that the riches of the land are confined. Soon, as a ridge that divides the southern- and eastern-flowing waters from those that discharge themselves into the Gulf of Carpentaria is crossed, other broader, longer, and still richer plains are entered upon. Away over to the Flinders river vast plains extend, over which a man might travel for a hundred miles either way without meeting with as many stones or pebbles as a farmer in the County Down picks from off his highly rented land every day in the year. Away beyond this undeveloped land lie the Plains of Promise, but these and other districts will have to be referred to further on.

Returning to the town of Bowen itself, we find it to be a most prosperous settlement near the mouth of the river Burdekin. Of the character of the country of which it is the port we have already spoken, as well as of the harbour near to which it stands. Bowen differs little in its general characteristics from many of the ports on the eastern coast to which reference has already been made. The English mail steamer from Singapore *viâ* Torres Straits makes this one of its calling-places, and communication with the other parts of the continent is kept up by a regular line of steam traders, besides many sailing vessels. It has its municipal council, of course; churches, educational institutes, and public-houses abound also as a matter of course; and, notwithstanding the constant opening up of other centres of population to the north and west, it is not likely to go back in the race for prosperity. That coal-mining will be one of the chief elements of this prosperity on the banks of the Burdekin there cannot be a doubt, for indications of large deposits of this mineral are sufficiently apparent in several directions.

Running up the country still farther north, the scenery becomes in parts still more tropical in character than that hitherto crossed over, whilst here and there the decidedly auriferous appearances of the land reminds the traveller of the more southern portions of **the continent.** Townsville, **the** first important settlement met with after leaving Bowen, may fairly be taken as an example of the rapidity with which communities spring up in Australia. It is situate on the shores of **Cleveland** Bay, having the Ross Creek running on its southern side. One advantage **it possesses that** will go far to make it the Ramsgate of Northern Queensland at some not distant day: **this is a** long stretch of sandy beach. Facing **this** beach the chief private residences and hotels are erected. It would be difficult **to** imagine a more favourable site for a town, and every day its natural advantages are being drawn upon. The harbour, if not a first-class one, is by no means to be despised: a long peninsula stretches out towards the sea, terminating in a somewhat bold headland known as Cape Cleveland, forming a capital protection to the bay itself. At one time the port promised to absorb the trade for the northern goldfields, but a town farther north, Cooktown, has rendered that pretty nearly impossible. In the course of its short life, however, Townsville has managed to send into the markets of the world fully twenty-four tons of gold, so "the potentiality of wealth" may be quite within its grasp yet.

To the west and north of Townsville gold and copper mining is pursued on a somewhat extensive scale. One of the most westerly towns of this part of the colony, Dalrymple, is situate in a very beautiful country, through which the Burdekin and several of its branches run. The river scenery here is of unusual beauty, the land bordering the various streams being exceedingly rich, but hitherto devoted to purely pastoral purposes. A memorial of the explorer Leichardt stands not far away from Dalrymple: it is a large gum-tree bearing the camping mark of that most ill-fated explorer. The country abounds in strange natural features; one of them, a sheer wall of basalt, extends across the country for several miles, and stands out well-defined and rampart-like from the surrounding country. It serves the **purposes** of a rampart too, for, being inaccessible to horsemen, the Blacks, **whenever** they have committed depredations that have called for reprisals, seek safety in the fastnesses, and bid defiance to their pursuers. Once entrenched behind this basalt barrier, the aboriginals can withstand every movement that can be made against them. From this it may be fairly inferred that the country enclosed by the rocky ridge abounds in the means of sustaining life. The character of this country has yet to be investigated and

described, for if white men have penetrated it, the knowledge they have obtained has been kept strictly private, and it is a veritable *terra incognita*. Farther west than Dalrymple, and away over the dividing range the Gilbert, the Etheridge, and farther west still, the Cloncurry gold-fields are met with. Not far from the latter, is the great Australian copper mine. Here are, perhaps, the richest deposits of copper in Australia; **and** when **the riches of** the Burra Burra and other mines in South **Australia are borne in mind, some** idea of the value of **the** Cloncurry fields may be had. **The** distance, however, of the mines from the seaboard has hitherto prevented their working; but the day is doubtless not far distant when the riches of the country will be fully developed; in the meantime, **some of the** richest gold of Australia has been obtained on **the** Cloncurry, **the** ultimate outlet for the trade of which will doubtless be **some** port in Carpentaria. The **Etheridge and** the Gilbert gold-fields **have both** been rich, and will doubtless continue so, although disaster has on more than **one** occasion attended the establishment of settlements in both districts. The discovery of gold farther north has been one of the chief causes of the comparative depression of the mines and consequent want of settlement in this quarter. Through this country the Queensland telegraph line, that up to reaching Cardwell—to which further reference will have to be made presently—had taken an almost due north course, runs to the westward until it finds its last terminus at Normantown, near the Gulf of Carpentaria.

Continuing the journey north, the main range of the colony closes **in** upon the coast, leaving little land available for settlement. **Opposite the mouth** of the Herbert river one of the most remarkable features of **the coast** of Queensland is met with; this is a bold precipitous island rising almost sheer up out of the water for fully three thousand feet. **Little is** known of it, but the voyager by sea who is brought within sight of it cannot fail to be struck with the grandeur of its proportions and picturesqueness of outline and feature. A somewhat remarkable point of land not far from **this has** received the appropriate name of Dungeness. There is some capital land and exquisite scenery on the banks of the Herbert, and sugar is being largely cultivated thereabouts. Running a northward course for another hundred **miles or** so, first **of** all Halifax, and then Rockingham Bay, are reached. Upon the shores of the latter, and nestling under the shade of one of **the** loftiest mountains in Queensland, the town of Cardwell is situate. Anything more charming than the position of this town it would be difficult **to** conceive. The background of mountains casts into bold relief, with **an** exceptional distinctness, the settlement and its surroundings. Here the scenery becomes intensely tropical in character. The lush luxuriance of the greenery of the hill-sides, valleys, and ravines compose a picture eminently pleasing to the eye and taste of the artist and ordinary journeyer. When first the gold diggings of the far north broke out, the future of Cardwell appeared a brilliant one. The bold back-line of hills, however, with which it is bounded on the west proved an almost insurmountable barrier between the town itself and the rich gold lands beyond; and Cooktown, still farther north, has inherited most of the good things once apparently intended for Cardwell. It possesses, however, natural riches in number sufficient to almost compensate for this. All the fruits and flowers of the tropics grow here with a luxuriance that many tropical countries have never known. The waters of the bay, too, abound in products of value. Here, among the green and delicate sea-herbage with which the shallow waters of the coast are lined, the dugong attains its greatest excellence. There is one little drawback to the marine treasures of the place: here, if anywhere in Queensland, the alligator finds its happiest hunting grounds. The bay abounds with them; and one old ill-looking brute is popularly known as the Cardwell pet. The name was doubtless given "sarcastic," as Artemus Ward would have said; but the existence of the alligator in considerable numbers on the shores and affluents of Rockingham Bay is a sufficiently well established fact. Inland, beyond the mountain range, the native Blacks have proved themselves to be almost, if not more troublesome than the long-jawed creatures of the coast. One other natural peculiarity of the place, and the journey north must be pursued with all possible rapidity: like some of the beaches on the coast of Cheshire, the beach of Cardwell abounds in fresh-water springs that perpetually bubble forth a wealth of limpid freshness, in some instances far below high-water mark. It would be impossible to over-estimate the value of such a supply of water in a country like Northern Queensland.

The next stage of the journey towards the far north takes both reader and author into a perfect *Prester John* country. Every schoolboy has heard of that long peninsula called by the name of York, that thrusts out its gradually-narrowing neck of land towards that mysterious island, New Guinea, in the concerns of which adventurers of every kind and character are so largely interested. At its extreme northern point, Cape York is considerably less than one hundred miles from the mainland of New Guinea. The latest instance of Australian development has been made at a point about half-way between Rockingham Bay and Cape York. Rightly

PARTE TASMANIA.

enough the settlement is named Cooktown, for **not** far from here brave Captain Cook threaded his way through the windings of the Great Barrier Reef and discovered a river, the which he named the Endeavour. On the banks of this river Cooktown is situate; and with brief allusion to it, this part of the world will have to be left with scant courtesy, so that other portions of the continent may be described. When the earlier pages **of** AUSTRALIA ILLUSTRATED were going through the press, Cooktown was unknown. What it is now, and what it is likely to become, will have to be told. The Etheridge and the Gilbert gold-fields have already been referred to. Prospectors from these fields discovered gold on the banks of the river Palmer, and a new world was opened not only to the gold-miner, but to the farmer and trader. The Cooktown of 1876 is perhaps as busy and prosperous a place as any on the Australian continent. Chinese muster in great numbers **not** only in Cooktown, but upon the diggings from which the importance of the place is derived. The Celestials enter into keen competition with the European traders, and in several instances they have given the highest prices for building sites in the town upon which to erect stores and hotels. The white man, the gold-digger especially, resents this intrusion, and taxes the almond-eyed ones pretty heavily; but in a country so well adapted to his nature he is sure to prosper, and prosperity has a powerful attraction for him. It will be interesting to watch the progress of Cooktown and its surrounding districts, if only because of the peculiarity attending its settlement in the matter of the admixture of races.

Beyond the **point** now arrived at, York Peninsula is an almost perfectly nondescript country. There are, to be sure, certain bays and headlands laid down on the maps, but beyond these and the appearance of certain parts of the mainland as seen from the sea, little is known. Besides the gold-fields and their attendant riches, some other valuable discoveries have been made. On the banks of the river Daintree a magnificent forest of cedar, extending for nearly a hundred miles on the course of that river, has given rise to great hopes as to its future value for trading purposes. At the extreme point of Cape York, some six hundred miles to the northward of Townsville, the small settlement of Somerset is situate, but save as a calling place for the mail-steamers from Singapore, there is little of interest attaching to it. Normanton, fully six hundred miles to the south—and this is the nearest point at which there is tangible ground for touching—possesses a special interest because of its being the northern termination of the Queensland telegraphic service. What the future of these latter settlements may be,

220   AUSTRALIA ILLUSTRATED.

it would be impossible to predict, but taking into consideration the distances at which they are placed, and the recent history of the districts by which they are bounded, a speedy prosperity may be anticipated for **them**.

Starting from Chesapeake, or Carpentaria, crossing and tracing up and **down the** rivers, lakes, expanses, and passing the spot where Burke first trod the rim, and left it to infest the waters of the north, and travelling through and across valleys and in some places tolerably elevated plains, the northern territory of South Australia is entered upon, and in the north-westerly corner thereof, Port Darwin, with the telegraph that has put its tolerably straight course from the far south nearly two thousand miles away, are met with. That Port Darwin may become the metropolis of the northern settlements is by no means impossible, although its past short career has evidenced many of the vicissitudes that accompany the formation of new districts in new countries. Great hopes were at one time entertained with reference to the future of Port Darwin, nor is there any very apparent reason why these hopes should not one day be realised. That it will yet become a second Singapore, those who most affect a belief in its future confidently affirm. As a harbour it presents advantages that cannot fail to enforce towards its ultimate prosperity. That it is admirably adapted for a shipping port for horses to India there cannot be a doubt, and now that the squatters of Queensland are beginning to shoot the wild horses with which many of their runs are infested, it may be that this trade may receive some attention. There are numerable inhabited islands lying to the north and west of Port Darwin, and with the natives of these a very considerable trade could be created. The coast hereabouts abounds with navigable rivers upon the banks and between which thousands of acres of soil of unusual richness await the toil of the husbandman. That gold, copper, tin, and many other metals exist in considerable quantities has been demonstrated over and over again, and that as the country is explored and opened up, other discoveries, not only of minerals but of land adapted for settlement will be made, may be taken for granted. The natural pastures are of unusual variety and richness even for Australia, and both horse and cattle stock arriving on the grazing grounds in poor condition, fatten rapidly. That this fact will give great value to Port Darwin as a shipping place for horses to India cannot be doubted.

TASMANIA

CHAPTER XXIV.
SOUTH AUSTRALIA, WESTERN AUSTRALIA, AND TASMANIA.

THE BORDER COUNTRY.—DESERTS.—A BASALT WALL.—AGRICULTURAL PRODUCTS.—WINE.—FRUITS.—TRADE.—TAXATION.—ROADS, RAILWAYS, AND TELEGRAPHS.—CHURCHES AND SCHOOLS.—ADELAIDE; ITS OLIVE GROVES; PUBLIC INSTITUTIONS.—GERMAN SETTLEMENTS.—ALDINGA.—MOUNT GAMBIER.—YORKES PENINSULA.—COPPER MINES.—PORT AUGUSTA.—THE WESTERN TELEGRAPH.—KING GEORGE'S SOUND.—JARRAH FORESTS.—PERTH AND FREEMANTLE.—TASMANIA.—HOBART TOWN.—LAKES AND MOUNTAINS.—THROUGH THE ISLAND.—LAUNCESTON.—CONCLUSION.

ALTHOUGH the two first-named colonies **standing at** the head of this chapter "run marches" with each other for more than **fourteen** hundred miles, there is a great barrier between them. Time after time have brave men attempted to pierce this barrier, and indeed they have succeeded, but the result of their success has in nearly every case been disappointment, and the tired hope begotten of vain endeavour has been the invariable result. Running down from the shores of Carpentaria to those of Spencer Gulf, traces **of this** endeavour and of its failure are to be met with at not unfrequent intervals. To the south and west of Central Mount Stuart the track taken by Major Warburton in 1875 is met with; farther south still the tracks of Forrest, Gosse, and Giles are crossed, but so far as the discovery of a practicable **route** from **one** colony to the other is concerned, the character of the country as **marked upon** the **maps and** described in the journals of the explorers, indicates **a succession of** arid, rocky plains; here and there patches of good land **have been** met with, but they are very few and far between. During the latter months of 1865, Mr. Ernest Giles, with a party of eight men and a score of camels, vainly endeavoured to find country worth having on the borders of the two colonies. He made a journey extending over five months, in the course of which 2,500 miles were traversed without discovering the wished-for pastures. At one stage of their wanderings the party travelled for sixteen days without meeting with a trace of water, there being fully 300 miles between one water hole and another. The whole aspect of the country was depressing in the extreme, animal life being almost entirely wanting, and the general features of the country tame and **monotonous. Once the wearying** sameness of the country was broken by a **far-extending wall of basalt, down** the perpendicular sides of which streams of water descended, some of them from a height of 200 feet, glittering in the bright sun as though...

> ...
> ...
> ...
> ...

As the ...... districts of South Australia are reached, although in a total ...... continent, the face of the country is changed. There are to be seen fewer bold and distant features in the landscape than in the other colonies, but at fully 130 miles from the southern coast signs of **the** richness of the land become plentiful enough; miles of corn-fields are met **with**, and pastures soon come **as the** world cannot equal. When South Australia was first settled, the idea **of cultivating** the land, that is, at any considerable distance from the coast, **was scouted and** laughed at. This has told its real Australian tale, and now South Australia is truly a land of corn, and oil, and wine. In the markets of the world, the wheat of South Australia is held in the highest possible esteem, and in Eastern Europe it is eagerly sought for as seed with which to improve the corn-lands of the Old World. From the crop of 1875-6 it was computed that 200,000 tons would be available for export. Its wine, too, is good as wine can be, and has already made its mark in the English market.

Foremost among those who have worked for the making of a market **for** Australian wines stands Mr. Patrick Auld, whose vineyard of Auldana is situate about four miles from the city of Adelaide, on one of the lower slopes of Mount Lofty, the most prominent object of the landscape around the capital of South Australia. Mr. Auld deserves credit not only for the foresight that in the early days of the colony led him to believe in the wine-growing capabilities of the land, but to endeavour, year after year, to make the produce worthy of the country. In order to effect this, he, early in the "seventies," visited the chief wine-making districts of Europe, and informed himself of the best methods of cultivating the vine, and the manipulation of the grape, for wine-making purposes. The result of this has been that the Auldana "ruby," and "white" occupies a very high position in the estimation of those whose knowledge and experience has enabled them to judge of the qualities of high-class wines. English physicians of repute put their faith to "Auldana," and many a weakening life has been strengthened by its use. It is only fair to say that Mr. Fallon, of Albury, New South Wales, has been equally persevering and successful in bringing into high

repute the wines of the valley of the Upper Murray. To return to the vintage of South Australia, however. In the season 1875-6, the cellars at the Auldana at the commencement of the latter year contained over 50,000 gallons of first-class wine. On the Beaumont vineyard 87,000 pounds of grapes were crushed; at Birksgate vineyard 5,000 gallons of wine were made; whilst at a vineyard quite close to Auldana, though still lower down the sides of Mount Lofty, Mr. Penfold produced 25,000 gallons of wine from 60 acres of vines; other vineyards were proportionately productive, and these results point out plainly a great wine-growing future for Australia. Oranges can hardly be kept from growing, whilst the various perfume-giving flowers of Europe and the East flourish with a luxuriance that their native countries know not of, and a large industry is awaiting development in connection therewith.

Some particulars with reference to agricultural labour and returns can hardly fail to prove interesting. In 1875, of the whole land under cultivation, two-thirds were devoted to wheat-growing, the exact number of acres being 839,638 acres, the product 9,803,693 bushels, giving an average of nearly twelve bushels to the acre. From 13,724 acres sown with barley, there was gathered 208,373 bushels of grain. To the oat crop there was devoted 2,785 acres, giving a yield of nearly 41,000 bushels. Of peas there were nearly 62,000 bushels gathered; whilst off 161,000 acres of land laid down for hay, there was reaped 203,000 tons of that article of forage. Of potatoes over 17,000 tons were dug from 4,600 acres of ground planted. The cultivation of this tuber is growing greatly in favour in the south-east corner of the colony, and the crop is nearly always a safe one. With reference to the cereals produced, it should be remembered that their cultivation is pursued for the most part after a very primitive fashion, and that, therefore, the cost of production leaves a good profit on the crops harvested. The olive, the almond, the mulberry, and scores of other valuable plants and trees grow with the slightest possible attention.

Statistics prepared towards the end of 1875 give some interesting and important particulars of the progress and position of South Australia. From these figures it appears that the population of the colony increased, from the year 1869 to 1874, from 180,000 to 204,000 persons. These had cultivated during the latter year nearly 1,130,500 acres of land, giving an average of seven acres per head of the population. The importation during the same year had amounted to £3,985,290, giving an average of £19 9s. per head. Against this the exports were stated at £4,402,855, or an average of

£31 10s. per head. The live-stock of the colony was: of horses 93,000, of cattle 185,000, and of sheep 6,120,000. The colony possessed also 570 miles of railways, and nearly 900 miles of main roads; whilst the electric telegraph reached 5,100 miles in length. This, of course, includes the line running to Port Darwin, in the northern territory.

While the material prosperity of the colony is thus so well assured, the religious, political, and social condition of the people is no less satisfactory. In connection with the first named, there are in the colony fully 620 places of worship, and about half that number of buildings occasionally used for religious purposes. South Australia has been called the colony of the sects, and a glance at the various denominations owning the churches and chapels referred to will go far to justify the name. Of recognised sections of the Church, there are enumerated members of the Church of England, and of the Roman Catholic Church—the first of these possessing 75, and the second 45 churches. In the matter of number of buildings, the Wesleyan Methodists more than double both these sects, for they boast of no less than 160 churches, and 120 other preaching places. In addition to this, they have nearly 200 Sunday schools, attended by some 15,000 scholars. The Baptists have 30, and the Presbyterians just half that number of churches. The Primitive Methodists possess 120 chapels, whilst the Bible Christians claim nearly 100. Besides these sects, there are the Christian Brethren, German Lutherans—these latter forming a highly important, interesting, and valuable portion of the population—members of the Society of Friends, Moravians, Unitarians, and Jews. The New Jerusalem Church has one place of worship, and the Methodist New Connection two. In connection with these facts and figures, indicative of so much prosperity, it may be as well to say that the South Australians are, in proportion to the privileges they enjoy, the most lightly taxed people in the world, for in 1869 the Colonial Treasurer estimated the taxation at £1 15s. $6\frac{1}{2}d$. per head per annum.

The capital of South Australia, the city of Adelaide, is, if not the most picturesque, at any rate one of the most prosperous and pleasant towns in the Australian colonies. It is, to be sure, subject to hot winds and dust-storms, but the dwelling-houses, places of business, and other buildings have, from almost the establishment of the colony, been constructed so as to afford the greatest possible protection against climatic peculiarities. The town is placed on a gently undulating plain of great fertility. Sufficiently near to form the most conspicuous objects in the landscape, the ranges of Mount Lofty stand

LONGFORD, TASMANIA.

out with a boldness and distinctness of outline that mountains of the same altitude in less favoured climes can rarely if ever possess. The city occupies a portion of both banks of a water-course named the Torrens, the north and south parts of the town being connected by two iron and two wooden bridges. The former are massive and somewhat imposing structures, and the whole of them answer the purposes for which they are designed efficiently **and well**. On the southern bank of the river the business portions of the city are situate, the north bank being chiefly devoted to private residences and gardens surrounding them. After the usual Australian fashion—that not a few visitors decry greatly, although it possesses many advantages—Adelaide is built on the principle of right angles. Many of the streets are planted on either side with trees, that have in not a few instances attained a considerable size. By-and-by the angular streets of Adelaide will present all the more pleasing features of the Boulevards of Paris, or, taking the character of the buildings into consideration, perhaps the streets and squares of Dusseldorf would convey a more life-like picture of the place to the European traveller and reader. The Torrens is not the Rhine, but the comparison here made **refers** to the streets and houses only, and not to the river. One point of superiority Adelaide may fairly claim over either of the cities to which it has just been compared : in many parts of the city and suburbs, Adelaide is a perfect olive grove ; these groves are not only beautiful to look at, but profitable to cultivate, and large quantities of olive oil of a superior character are now produced from the fruit of the trees of the gardens attached to the houses of the citizens. This "mine on the surface of the earth," as an olive grove is called in Spain, may in all probability prove as valuable to South Australia as has its copper mines, or perhaps the wool-clip itself—wine and oil are not likely to run a losing race even with wool and copper. Adelaide is the oldest municipality in Australia, and the varied benefits of this system of local government are fully manifest in the sanitary and social state of the city. The Post Office is a building of which any city might be proud. In common with the majority of the chief edifices of the place, it is built of a peculiarly fine white freestone, and this gives a lightness and cheerfulness of aspect to the place, that the brick of Sydney or the bluestone of Melbourne fails to bestow. As may have been anticipated from what has been said of the other towns of the Australian colonies, the social, religious, and literary institutions of Adelaide are all of an important and thoroughly useful character. The houses of parliament and government offices have all been conceived and carried out in a liberal and even a munificent spirit. The same characteristic applies to

the South Australian Institute, with which is connected an elaborately
arranged museum, and a carefully selected library of nearly 20,000 volumes.
The hospital has accommodation for over 200 patients; besides the hospital
there are several other institutions of a benevolent character. Churches
and chapels are to be met with in every direction, whilst good hotels
are by no means difficult to find. The town is well lit with gas, and the
water-supply, received from large and well-constructed reservoirs a few
miles from the town, is all that could be desired. As in Melbourne,
Sydney, and Brisbane, the botanic gardens form by no means an unimportant feature in the attractions of the city, and a park adjoining them is
growing year by year in attractiveness and beauty. There are four daily and
half-a-dozen weekly newspapers published in the town, the latter including a
German, an Irish, a Church of England, and a Methodist journal. All round
about the city are villages, or suburbs as they are called, favourite places of
residence with those engaged in the city, and with which constant and convenient communication is kept up by numbers of cars and omnibuses. There
remains only space to add that the population numbers over 50,000 persons,
inhabiting nearly 8,000 houses.

Besides Adelaide, there are a good many important towns and centres of
population in South Australia, but lack of space demands that reference to
them should only be of the briefest. South of the city, there first comes the
pretty little summer resort of Glenelg, and farther south still, the German
settlement of Hahndorf, in the neighbourhood of which, gold has been found
in payable quantities; but the chief riches of the place consist of wheat,
potatoes, and grapes, the whole of which are assiduously cultivated by the
honest hard-working German inhabitants, who number some five hundred.
A German settlement of much the same size, Lobethal by name, lies amid
some pleasant and indeed romantic hills near the Onkaparinga river, whilst
a smaller settlement is met with at Rosenthal, near the beautiful Barossa
ranges. Farther south than Hahndorf, silver and lead mines have been
worked near the village of Talisker. Aldinga is a prosperous little town, and
is held in high favour by newly married couples during their honeymoon.
It has a fine beach, beautiful surroundings, and the climate is delightful.
Mount Gambier, situate at the far southern corner of the colony, is by far the
most important of the south-eastern towns. An extinct volcano, after which
the town is named, is the most prominent object of the country, the whole of
which is a rich agricultural one. Indeed, nearly the whole of the country
enclosed by the Victoria boundary, intersected by the river Murray, and

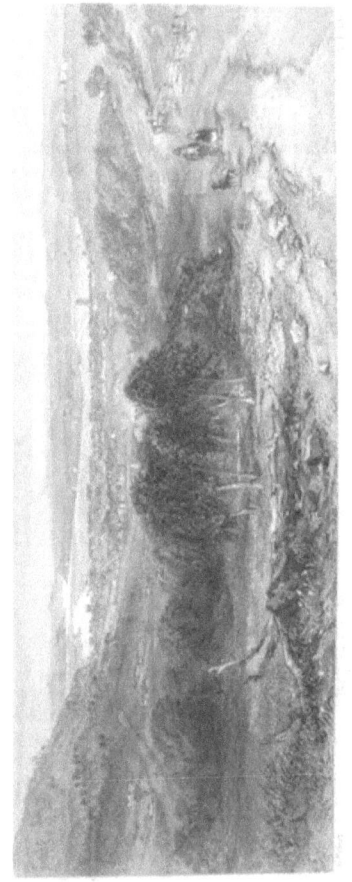

LAUNCESTON, TASMANIA.

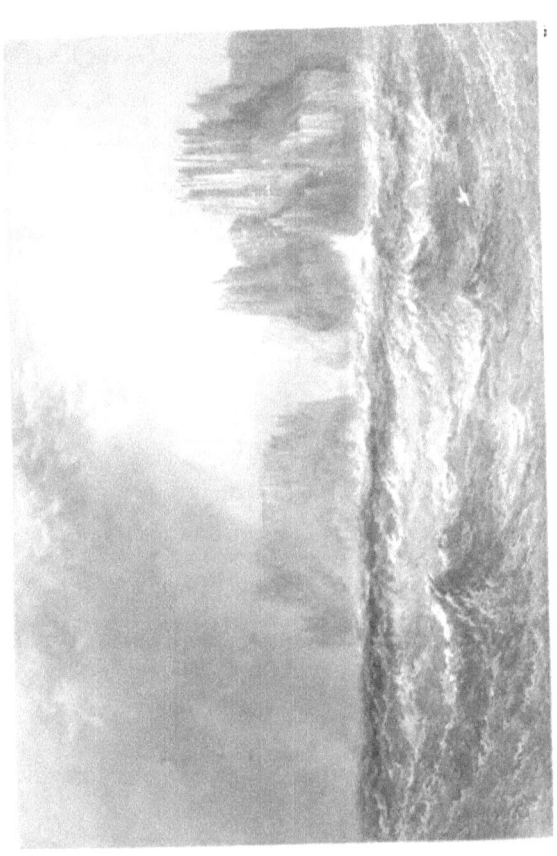

having Gulf St. Vincent for its western side, may be **described in similar terms.** Across the gulf, Yorkes Peninsula stretches away towards Kangaroo **Island, and at the** northern end of the peninsula the copper workings of **Moonta, Kadina, and** Wallaroo are situate. These mines, although discovered long after the famous Burra Burra, have far exceeded it **in** richness. The story of the treasure discovered hereabouts sounds almost fabulous, but mines worked without the necessity of a single shilling of capital being subscribed, and resulting in money gains to the extent of millions of money, must have a strong foundation of fact to support them. In the January of 1876 a new and exceedingly rich lode of copper was discovered at a greater depth than any previous workings, so that the mineral riches of South Australia are positively incalculable.

Piercing into the land for more than double the distance of the Gulf of St. Vincent, Spencer Gulf offers the most southerly port of South Australia proper. This is Port Augusta; and as Port Darwin is declared to be the coming Singapore of Australia, so Port Augusta is designated as the future New Orleans: that it is admirably situate is patent. The port is a good one, and the country to the north, east, and west, rich in grasses and minerals. From Port Augusta, several exploring expeditions have started for the purpose of penetrating into Western Australia; with what success has been already shown. From this point also, another departure of interest has taken place: the electric telegraph between Adelaide and Western Australia here has its commencement. From Port Augusta to Port Lincoln, the line **runs nearly** parallel with the western shore of Spencer Gulf; from Port Lincoln, it follows as nearly as may be the track taken along the shores of the Great Australian Bight, in 1840, by the explorer Eyre: this track conducts over the boundary line between South and Western Australia. Even were space remaining, there is little to be said of this part of Australia. Low sandy levels, here and there grassy plains, varied by a very occasional rise and sparsely timbered forests, characterise the route. The country is uninteresting in the extreme, the only point of interest being Albany, situate on King George's Sound; and the only interest attaching to the town, although in the year 1876 it was exactly half a century old, is derived from the **fact of** the Peninsular and Oriental mail-steamers calling for coaling purposes at the port. It would be difficult to conceive a place less likely to impress a fresh arrival with the capabilities and advantages of Australia than the country he would see on landing at Albany.

That the "curse of convictism" is not an unmitigated evil, is indicated

228 AUSTRALIA ILLUSTRATED.

after a very special ..... by a road made entirely by convict labour, running through the whole weary waste of over 260 miles that lie between Albany and Perth, the capital of the colony. Forests of jarrah, broken here and there by clumps of sandalwood, are the chief features of the country. The jarrah is certainly one of the handsomest trees of the Australian continent; it grows to a great size, and when cut at the proper season its timber, so far as all experience goes, is absolutely indestructible—white-worms or water-worms are powerless in their attacks upon it, and had the "wooden walls" of Old England not gone out of fashion it would be invaluable for marine purposes. In the construction of the Indian railways it has been used to the greatest possible extent for sleepers, and no instance ..... of them having decayed or given way is reported. The jarrah forests are practically illimitable, and will prove a source of wealth for ages to come. The sandal-wood is used for purposes very different to those to which the jarrah is applied—instead of making good, honest, and serviceable railway sleepers, wharf piles, ships, and houses, it is taken to China and there offered as a burnt sacrifice to the joss of Celestial worshippers. Corn and wood are produced plentifully in Western Australia, but, next to the jarrah forests, the pearl fisheries mostly attract the adventurous and enterprising. It only requires that gold should be added to the "baritone pearl" to make Western Australia a very rich country indeed.

Perth, the chief town of the colony, and the seat of government,—the form of which differs from that of all the other colonies, inasmuch as it has not yet been granted the privilege of a constitution, nor do the majority of the colonists appear very desirous of possessing the boon,—is pleasantly positioned on the shores of Melville Water, a long and wide reach of the Swan, and about twelve miles from the mouth of that river. This Melville Water is thoroughly lake-like in its character, the far apart extremities closing in the scene on either side. Mount Eliza is one of the most prominent features in the scene. The cliffs are fully 100 feet high, and almost perpendicular, the water washing the base with the gentlest of motions. The landward side of Mount Eliza is undulating, and upon the slopes many of the citizens of Perth have built their residences, the house of the bishop being perhaps the best of them. The city lies in full view on the level land below, the intervening space being filled with well-grown trees and flowering shrubs. Fringing the river, forests of banana and bamboo mark the water-line, whilst the gardens surrounding the houses are rich in orange and lemon-trees, other fruits and flowers being plentifully mingled with them.

CATARACT GLEN, MOUNT WELLINGTON, TASMANIA.

Flowers are the great glory of Perth, and, indeed, of the whole of the settled districts of Western Australia. Looking from the elevation of the mount overlooking the town, the hills of the Darling range (the main range of the colony) close in a very beautiful panorama in that direction.

The streets of the city are wide, and being lined on either side with Cape lilacs has, lacking the continuous rows of houses, a good deal the appearance of a boulevard. In nearly all the streets shops alternate with private houses, and in not a few instances open spaces and gardens secure to the inhabitants a plentiful supply of fresh air. Chief among the public buildings stands the City Hall, a building affording accommodation to the legislative council and other public bodies, the basement of the whole being used as a market. Protestants and Catholics have each a cathedral of their own. The English cathedral is plain almost to ugliness; the Catholic building sufficiently good-looking, but far surpassed by the place of worship erected by the Wesleyans; various other denominations have churches and chapels. There is a literary institute and museum in the town, an excellent club, and good hotels. The majority of the houses are built either of stone or brick, and when the drainage of the city has been attended to, Perth will be a really pleasant city to live in. It already possesses a population of 5,000, including the military and convicts, these two latter numbering some 400.

Freemantle, the chief port of the colony, is situate at the mouth of the Swan River, and about twelve miles from Perth, with which place it is connected by a capitally-made road and the electric telegraph. The port is a poor one, but by-and-by, when a certain "harbour bar" is removed, there will be nothing much to desire in this respect. The most conspicuous object in Freemantle is a huge ugly building standing on the top of a hill, and forming the "establishment" for convicts. Freemantle is by no means a lively-looking town; that mass of masonry on the hill, and the purposes to which it is applied, does not tend to make matters more cheerful. The beach, with its background of flowers, the former snow-white, and the latter glowing and glorious in all the colours flowers can possibly assume, helps to relieve the dulness of the scene; but nothing save busy men, with the various industries they pursue, can ever make Freemantle a cheerful place. Off the coast, and of course towards the west, lies the by no means elegantly named Rottnest Island, the marine residence of the Governor of the colony. Closer inland is Garden Island and many others, having peculiar beauties and attractions of their own. Besides the "establishment" already referred to, there are various other public buildings. First of all comes Government

House, and then an Oddfellows' Hall, this latter serving also the purposes of a municipal council chamber. Of course there are a number of churches, several schools, more than an equal number of hotels, and a very fine wooden bridge, 1,000 feet long, spanning the river Swan.

There are several other towns and centres of population, more or less large, lying north, east, and south of Perth, but none of them calling for special notice. Away up in the north there are Geraldtown and Northampton, and between these two towns the only railway hitherto constructed in the colony runs. Farther north still is the head-quarters of the pearl fisheries; but the surroundings of nearly all these places are of a common-place description. Inland, that is to say, approaching to and running over the Darling range, are many beautiful bits of scenery, pleasant water-courses, valuable forests of timber; and good land, although in scattered patches, sufficiently abounds to suffice for the profitable settlement of hundreds of thousands of people. One of the most prosperous of these districts is named York. It lies fully 60 miles to the east of Perth; nearly 3,000 persons are settled there, and they have brought over 10,000 acres of land under cultivation, the half of which is devoted to the growing of wheat. There only remains space to add that the whole of this immense colony possesses a population numbering little over 25,000 persons, fully half a score nationalities being represented.

A hundred and twenty miles south of the Australian continent lies Tasmania, and within its borders are to be found all the beauties of natural scenery, wealth of products, and salubrity of climate intensified and added to, of the colonies on the mainland. Tasmania is as nearly as possible the same size as Ireland; and in many of their aspects, social and physical, the two islands possess a similarity one to the other. If Ireland is the "first gem of the sea," Tasmania may fairly claim to be the "pearl of the Pacific." Words are powerless to express the charms of the natural scenery of the island. Nature would appear to have designed that within its narrow bounds all the desirable belongings of the great island continent should be reproduced on this little spot of land. It has been briefly described "as a beautiful well-watered island, rich in harbours and inlets, traversed by high mountain chains, full of crags, glens, and ravines of commanding appearance, the basaltic cliffs of some being several hundred feet in perpendicular height. The coast offers the most manifold changes and generally charming scenery. The interior is especially delightful, uniting the climate of Italy, the beauty of the Apennines, and the fertility of England." No description in words, however, could do justice to the natural beauties of Tasmania; but fortunately,

LAKE ST CLAIR, VA

where the pen of the writer fails the pencil of the artist is available, and the engravings of Tasmania with which this work is enriched will give a far more vivid idea of the country than any written description could do. Take as an example the sequence of pictures commencing with Lake St. Clair. Nestled in the bosom of hills nearly 4,000 feet above the sea, into which its waters flow, its shores and surroundings present an ever-varying variety of scenery. From this lake the river Derwent issues, its head waters being admirably portrayed in the engraving entitled "The Source of the Derwent." Then we have "The Derwent" itself, and the picture will at once convey a lively idea not only of the natural beauty of the river but of its home-like surroundings. The "queer, quaint" old homestead, the modern house in the distance, the quiet lake and the boldly-defined hills beyond, form a perfect picture of the place. The view of Hobart Town shows the Derwent about a dozen miles from its entrance into the waters that flow on and on to far beyond the South Pole without a single foot of known land to break its current. The foreground of the view of Hobart Town shows the homestead of the ordinary farmer and labourer, then comes the bay with its yachts, and steam and trading vessels, then the well-looking capital of Tasmania; beyond, Mount Wellington rises 4,000 feet high, with its top "cloud-capped" often, and not unfrequently snow-capped also." The view of "The Quay at Hobart Town" exhibits a pleasing phase of the labour-life of the capital. There are some twenty thousand people, and about five thousand houses, in Hobart Town proper. The public buildings form the chief features of the city. There are nearly two score churches and chapels in the town, and they are all well attended. Government House may be fairly described as a palace, for it is truly palatial in its appearance and in reality also. It would be difficult to imagine an appliance of high civilization that is not more than satisfactorily represented in and around Hobart Town. It would be esteemed a model town in any part of the world, and in addition to ordinary advantages it has others peculiar to itself. One fact may here be noted that is really noteworthy: after years of patient toil, chiefly undertaken by Mr. J. A. Youl, the fact of real English salmon having been perfectly acclimatised in Tasmania was, on the first day of 1876, demonstrated by the unmistakable fact of fully one hundred salmon being caught in the Derwent, not far from Hobart Town.

From Hobart Town in the south to Launceston in the north part of the Island there runs a road every mile of which presents new beauties and creates fresh interests. The old home fashions and appearances continually present themselves. The road itself is as perfect as road can be, its immediate boundaries being hedgerows of the English hawthorn, wild rose, honeysuckle, besides innumerable native flowers and shrubs of exceeding beauty. Farms are met with all along the road, from which there runs innumerable valleys, each possessing its own permanent water-course, the bright and sparkling waters serving to render the comparison with Ireland the more complete. Although things have been improving of late years, the farms have a decidedly Irish appearance. During the early years of the gold discoveries in Victoria and New South Wales farming in Tasmania was conducted after a very primitive fashion. Seeds were sown and crops reaped year after year, but there the care bestowed upon the land ended, and exhaustion of the soil naturally followed. Land, however, was plentiful and cheap, and new farms were taken up in preference to improving the old ones; many of these lay fallow for so long that their original richness returned, and now they are again being cultivated in a fashion more in accordance with the changed state of things. A railway now runs through the island, following to a great extent the line of the old road; and this, of course, adds to the facilities for the profitable opening up of the country. There are several towns on the line of road, the first of them being Richmond, most pleasantly situate on the Coal river. Oatlands is a busy little town, and so is its neighbour Cornwallis. Before arriving at Launceston the village of Perth is passed through, and then one of the most picturesque roads in the world has been travelled over. Launceston takes second rank among the towns of the colony; it is situate at the junction of the North and South Esk rivers, which here form the Tamar, running by this name forty miles to the sea. The town is enclosed by hills and is a busy, prosperous, and good-looking place. There are nearly one hundred settled towns in Tasmania, the whole of them possessing features calling for special notice, but such notice cannot be given here.

Besides the main island there are between fifty and sixty others included within the colony; some of these are inhabited, and interesting colonies are to be found on them. The engraving showing Tasman's Island will serve to give readers a vivid idea of the grandeur of some of the scenery on the coast, whilst the other illustrations will serve the same good turn for the more salient features of the country. It only remains to say that to do full justice to the beauty of Tasmania would require space not here available; it is indeed a very beautiful place, and one that should command greater attention from seekers for new homes than it has hitherto done, and we part with it after so brief a notice with regret.

www.ingramcontent.com/pod-product-compliance
Lightning Source LLC
Chambersburg PA
CBHW020918230426
43666CB00008B/1488